American Girl

American Girl

Scenes from a
Small-Town
Childhood

Mary Cantwell

Random House New York

Library of Congress Cataloging-in-Publication Data
Cantwell, Mary.
American girl : scenes from a small-town childhood
America / Mary Cantwell. —1st ed.
p.   cm.
ISBN 0-394-57502-4
1. Cantwell, Mary—Childhood and youth.   2. Bristol (R.I.)—
Biography.   3. Bristol (R.I.)—Social life and customs.   I. Title.
F89.B8C36   1992
974.5'5042'092—dc20
[B]   91-51021

Manufactured in the United States of America
2 4 6 8 7 5 3
First Edition

The text of this book is set in Linotype Walbaum

Book design by Lilly Langotsky

FOR THE FAMILY
THAT LIVED AT 232 HOPE STREET

American Girl

Preface

I started telling the stories a long time ago because they gave color and shape to someone who, for a while, was invisible to herself. She was a young woman who lived in New York and was married to a young man who looked a lot like Montgomery Clift. But the young woman couldn't locate herself either in New York City or in her marriage. It was only when she talked about the town in which she grew up that she could find her place on the map.

Every morning this young woman got out of bed, dressed and walked a few blocks with her husband to a corner where they waited for the Madison Avenue bus. Before she took the elevator to her office (she was a secretary on a fashion magazine) she waited on line in the coffee shop downstairs for a blueberry muffin and black coffee. The muffin stuck to the roof of her mouth and she would never really like coffee, but breakfast at one's desk seemed to her a New York thing. She wanted very much to do the New York thing.

At noon she wandered through stores like Blooming-dale's and B. Altman for white sale sheets and blankets, and at night she stopped at a grocery store for Kraft's Seven-Minute Macaroni Dinner and the occasional veal scallopini. She had no idea how to cook except from a book her husband had given her called *Quick and Easy Meals for Two.* But he liked everything she turned out: He was serious about domesticity. She was not serious about anything because no one thing struck her as any more important than any other.

When they went to bed she took off her wedding ring before turning off the lamp and pulling up the sheets. That way she could forget that she had committed herself to a lifetime under the body that, like clockwork, turned to hers the minute the light was out. In the morning her husband looked at her from eyes in which hurt and trust were inextricably and permanently mixed, and she sees them now as sharply as she did then.

But all that is another tale, and one that's too painful to tell. In any case it comes down to just one sentence: In marrying that particular young man that young woman had traveled too far from home.

That was, as I said, a long time ago. But I go on telling the stories, though now I tell them only to myself. A silly habit, I suppose, but there it is. On insomniac nights my lips move and a soundless voice says "One day Ganny and I were walking toward the drygoods store when . . ."

Chapter One

Around six o'clock of a Friday afternoon, three or four weekends a year, I travel the subway from Times Square to Penn
Station. If it is summer, and it usually is, the stairs down to
the hole in the ground are ripe with the stench of urine. I
clutch the railing hard and stiffen my shoulders, prepared
for the shove in the back, the grab at the purse, and my eyes
are everywhere and nowhere. It isn't wise to be caught looking at anybody in Times Square, and even less wise not to
be looking at everybody. Sooner or later in New York one
learns the trick of the blind, all-seeing gaze.

The subway is jammed and so is the lower level of Penn
Station, where the commuters are flowing toward the
stripped-down, sliding-door trains that will take them to
Long Island and backyard cookouts. The upper level, with
its long curve of ticket windows and big waiting room, is
jammed too, but not necessarily with travelers. Some people
are simply waiting out the day, and night, their backs to the
signboard. But I'm watching it, watching for The Merchants

Limited   Track 13   On Time   and the dispatcher's sonorous "Stopping at Rye, Stamford, Bridgeport, New Haven, New London, Kingston, Providence, Route 128, and South Station, Boston."

When the train is announced I move with the speed of long practice and zigzag down the dingy iron stairs to the platform. Within minutes I find a seat, shove my bag into the overhead rack, put on my reading glasses (I have only just acquired them) and bury myself in a book. I have traveled a great deal, and almost always alone, so I am adept at settling in, getting comfortable.

Oblivious to the tunnel and fleeting Westchester and the frequenters of the lavatories and the café car who lurch up and down the aisles, I read until New Haven, where the train halts while it goes from diesel to electric. Or is it from electric to diesel? The lights go out then, and there is nothing to do but stare out the window at the posters for Broadway shows and try to picture where those who are getting off are going.

I might have lived in New Haven: When I was nineteen I had a boyfriend there. He had fair hair and a camel's-hair polo coat, a heavyweight's shoulders and a hound's thirst, and when he danced his feet skimmed the floor. My children can't believe that a woman, a girl, like me, could ever have liked a man, a boy, like him. He doesn't seem, could never have been, their bookish mother's type. But, then, they never saw the width of his shoulders in his camel's-hair coat, or the lazy stretch of his long gray-flannel legs.

We have been traveling about an hour and a half now, and as far as I'm concerned the trip—though it isn't literally so—is halfway over. Because once we leave New Haven we will be entering my country.

Except in June, when wild red roses reach toward the tracks, my country is somber when seen from the windows of a train. The landscape is sepia-toned and the water that laps the occasional stretch of lonely beach is a dull, dense blue. The houses are small and sober. Those near the beaches are standing on stilts and those in the hollows have above-ground pools. Those nearest the tracks have roller shades at the windows, and limp curtains. Where there are trees they are up to their shins in ferns, and where there are reeds it is muddy, and there are waterfowl.

The traffic in the aisles is a trickle now. Many of the passengers are dozing, their heads wedged into odd and impossible corners. But I am wide awake, straining to see beyond the glass, beyond the night. Ah, the train is moving again, the lights are on, a few people have returned to their books. Not I. This is where I start to count milestones.

Here's Old Saybrook and its long, low bridge—I sailed under that bridge once—and here's New London. "Look," I would say if I had anyone to say it to, "look up there to the left. See that tall smokestack? That's where I went to college." In an oatmeal-colored tweed suit with silver buttons, from Best & Company.

The trains were nicer in those days, and had dining cars with slick starched tablecloths and bud vases. Their tiny kitchens served what everybody said was the best broiled scrod you could get anywhere, and ice cubes clinked in the sweaty silver pitchers. This train has no dining car, no glassed-off sections in which businessmen and secretaries off on a toot can drink old-fashioneds and smoke till the air is blue. Now all anybody drinks is diet soda and New York State wine in screw-top bottles, and there's a crumpled potato-chip bag in every other seat pocket.

The train is picking up speed, or maybe it is I who am picking up speed, and the stations are becoming blurs. Here's Westerly—there used to be a good ice-cream place in Westerly—and South Kingston, where my sister went to school, and Wickford, which is rich and boaty. Here's the Gorham Silver plant, and a huge, flat-roofed store called Ann and Hope, and here's the scattering of gawky multi-family clapboards that is New England's way of announcing urban sprawl. Another hour or so and I will be in what mothers from time immemorial have called "your own little bed."

The train is slowing down, the conductor has pinned back the doors between cars, and a few of the passengers, half-asleep, are taking down their Samsonites and duffels and garment bags. It's time to disembark, time to walk down a long steep hill in a city that is always choked with damp to a bus shelter that stands lighted and lonely in front of City Hall. It's late, and I will be on the last bus of the evening.

Sometimes kids are sitting in the back of the bus drinking from beer cans stashed in paper bags, hilarious after a night on the town. But for the most part the passengers are regulars heading home at the end of the late shift, who greet the driver familiarly and stare sleepily through the window as the bus swings out of the station. One by one they are dropped off at corners and gas stations and bus shelters in the middle of nowhere. " 'Night," they call back to him as they step off into the dark. " 'Night," he calls out after them.

We have traveled about seventeen miles, through flat fields and solitary houses and sudden spreads of water, when, at last, we cross a kind of causeway. On the right a harbor is glinting darkly; on the left a pond is silver as a coin. The trees close in and hide the harbor, and after several blocks of houses, Victorian mostly, a white marble school building and a mansion behind a long, wrought-iron fence, we enter a small business district. There are no lights in any of the stores, no passersby, and few cars. A blink, and we're out of it, and the trees have closed in on us again.

It's near midnight now and the bus is almost empty. Wait! There's my stop, that corner, beside the brick wall. I pull the cord, collect my bag and walk to the front of the bus, fearful the driver will go right past it. The brakes shudder, the door whumps, and I step off into air that smells like the air coming off the Hudson. Only this air is ten times saltier and has a green top note.

Across the street a light is burning over a doorway reached by a tall flight of stairs. The house, too, is tall, and white, and riding peacefully at anchor. Downstairs is dark: My aunt, who is serene in the belief that I am sure to get there, wherever "there" may be, has been asleep for hours. Upstairs, however, is blazing from stem to stern. My mother, who has no such certainty, is thumbing through a magazine, ears pricked for the sound of the bus as it hurtles toward Newport, and the abrupt wheeze that tells her it's stopped to let somebody off.

Behind me the harbor is whispering softly, and above me the trees are rattling in a light breeze. I look cautiously to the left and to the right—at this hour there's little traffic, but you never know—and as I do I feel my body growing lighter by many years, many pounds. The breeze is lifting them off and carrying them out over the water—out past Hog Island and Prudence Island and all the way to Narragansett Bay. I sling my bag over my shoulder, breathe deeply of the brine and cross the street. No longer am I the middle-aged woman who descended those subway steps 200 miles ago. I am Mary Lee Cantwell, and I am the child of this house.

Chapter Two

In my parents' wedding photograph my mother is smiling toothily from underneath an enormous horsehair hat and her bouquet is dripping stephanotis and small bows. Her sister, Esther, is also wearing a big hat and carrying a big bouquet. My father and his best man, a boyhood friend named George Driscoll, are wearing striped trousers; a grape arbor is directly behind them. Milling about somewhere outside the frame are the bride's parents, whom I will call Ganny and Gampa, the groom's mother, whom I will never know, his brothers and sisters, and assorted guests. Before this day is over one of the guests will suffer the splash of a pear on his head.

I have seen that picture many times, but never as clearly as I see one that exists only in my mind. It is of Leo Cantwell and Mary Lonergan at one o'clock of a weekday afternoon, standing on the town common of Bristol, Rhode Island. Leo is on his lunch hour from the U.S. Rubber Company; Mary is on her lunch hour from the Walley School, where she teaches third grade; and they are courting.

They were introduced, at Leo's request (he had seen Mary at a Yacht Club dance) by Esther, who also works at the rubber factory. Marriage is inevitable. She, after all, is a pretty Catholic girl and he is an up-and-coming Catholic boy. Actually, they are not kids—he is twenty-five and she twenty-six when they marry—but never mind. Both are innocent.

They are also very different from each other. Mary is shy and self-contained and high-strung. She grew up in a place where to be Irish is to be second-class, and she trusts the designation. Leo will have none of that. He is the son of a Glasgow man, a soldier in the Scots Guards, and a tall Irishwoman with snapping black eyes, and he has no awe of such as Mayflower descendants. "Imagine!" I will hear him say, "just because that bird's great-great-grandfather had a livery stable in Bristol in 1818 he thinks he's royalty. Hah!" And when, knowing children whose ancestors' names are in my history books, I ask whom I'm descended from, he will say "You're descended from me, and don't you forget it."

But that is later, many years later, and Mary and Leo are still standing on the dusty, dun-colored Common. I can see the gold chain that swags his stomach and the blue-and-gold enamel watch, a Christmas present from him, that hangs on the chain around her neck, but I can only guess at their conversation. Perhaps he is telling her about how some of the gay blades who live at the Belvedere Hotel—young men like him, from out of town, moving up the executive ladder at U.S. Rubber—went down to the kitchen last night to take potshots at the rats. Maybe he's inviting her to the movies, or maybe Esther has found a new speak. "Every time they raided a blind pig," he will tell me one day, "they found your Aunt Esther sitting in the middle of it." Not that Esther is a tosspot, oh no, but she is lively, so lively that soon she will travel to New York for Rudolph Valentino's wake.

Or perhaps it is all settled between them, and they have exhausted the Yacht Club dances and the picnics at Colt Farm and the shore dinners at Rocky Point and are talking about a dining-room table. Perhaps they are deciding on the mahogany bedroom set from Cherry & Webb and whether the silver should be Gorham, as is everyone else's, because the company's in Rhode Island. (And, yes, it will be Gorham. Fairfax, to be exact.)

Anyway, one hot August morning they are married, in the basement of St. Mary's Church because its Gothic superstructure isn't finished yet. Gampa, tall, skinny, not as shrewd as his brothers and sisters but the only one of them, Papa says, who has a heart, gives the bride away. The groom is taking her to New York for their honeymoon, on the old Fall River Line. It is Prohibition so I don't know about the liquid refreshments, but since one of Gampa's brothers owns a hotel and Gampa himself once owned a bar, I suspect there is alcohol present. If there is, no drop will pass Ganny's lips.

The photographer summons the bride and groom. Leo, Mary, Esther, and George line up. A breeze stirs the lawn in front of the grape arbor. The August sun is like a hammer. Behind the bridal party, on one of the two trees beyond the arbor, a pear—a pear about which my parents will tell me and I will tell my children and my children will tell theirs because it stamps this day into the family memory more surely than a photograph—is poised for the drop.

On the night before the May morning I was born, my father sat on the front steps of our house on Bradford Street, smoking a Fatima and watching the sun set into Bristol Harbor.

Bristol Harbor is enclosed by two claws—a big claw, which is the town itself, and a little claw called Poppasquash Point—and sailboats dance on it in summer. Lobster boats plow through it all year round and so does the dumpy Prudence Island ferry.

There are two islands in the harbor, Hog and Prudence, and people live on them when the weather's warm, in rackety houses with outdoor plumbing. Once past Prudence, which is the biggest and the farthest out, the harbor sweeps into Narragansett Bay. So, pouring from the east side of the big claw, does Mount Hope Bay, which separates us from

Massachusetts. Bristol people tend to be long-lived. Some say it's the brine that keeps them.

While Papa smoked and studied the sunset, my mother and her widowed Aunt Annie were on the telephone, turning the town upside down to find him. Neither thought to look out the window. Finally he finished his Fatima, stood up, stretched and walked inside. "Leo," my mother said. "You'd better call Horse Lanoue."

Horse Lanoue. Never was there such a town for nicknames as Bristol. Among my parents' contemporaries are Bink, Fruit Face, Skeet, Kitty Eyes, Bumper, Twister, Punk, Poop, Crackers, Peanuts, Pinhead, Funnybird, Beanie, Silent Sid, and Hungry Frank. Among mine will be Zip, Fat, Tweet, Eppie, Nutsy, and Gut.

Mother got into Horse's car—Papa didn't have one—and Papa followed, slinging her small suitcase into the front seat. Off they went, up to the corner of High and Bradford streets, where Horse made a left. Meanwhile, Aunt Annie, who was lame, limped her way toward 232 Hope Street, where Ganny and Gampa had given her the hall bedroom, with the news. And I, eyes closed, limbs flailing, still cozy in the amniotic sac, began my tour of what was to become my territory. My country.

High Street is broad and leafy, and goes from ship-owner's Federal at its south end to millhand's three-decker at the north. The big gray Congregational Church, outside which I will wait to eye the bride and her bridesmaids on

Saturday afternoons, is on High Street, along with the sober stone mansion that is its parish house. So, until some nitwit tore it down a few years ago, was a curious triangular building that had housed some of Lafayette's troops and been sledged across the ice from Poppasquash Point after the Revolution. One learns about history early in Bristol, simply by looking around.

A left, then a right, and the travelers were on Hope Street, passing Guiteras Junior High—the gift of the descendants of a rich Cuban planter and my future alma mater—and heading for the Neck. That's the name for the north end of town. They passed Fort Hill, where Lafayette set up his command post and where the Cantwell girls will go sledding, and Collins Pond, where they will ice skate, and Colt Farm, through which the elder, along with Ruthie and Joan and Jeanne and Anne (none of them here yet but all of them in progress), will take long Sunday afternoon walks.

They passed a house that was built in 1680 (Bristol's first church services were held here), a rambling red clapboard in which Lafayette spent a night, a two-room school, dairy farms, a few bungalows, a house ordered from a Sears, Roebuck catalogue, and the estate of a woman who was born America's richest baby. And they drove, as one does everywhere in Bristol, under a canopy of oak, horse chestnut, maple and, until the Dutch disease got them, elm trees.

Was my mother nervous? Of course. This was her first confinement. Was my father excited? He wanted six children, all of them female. What about Horse? He was saying things like "Won't be much longer, Mary," and "Nothing to worry about, Leo."

Over the town line they went and into Warren, where my mother's father came from; through Barrington, at whose annual Thanksgiving Day football game with Colt Memorial High School their daughters will suffer chills and muddy feet; through dreary Riverside and into Providence with its stinking river and its steep hills. A few hours later I will be born, at Lying-In Hospital, and in a few years I will not forgive my parents this journey. Their bringing me to Providence to be born means that, unlike my mother and grandmother and great-grandmother, I am not, strictly speaking, a Bristolian.

It's probably different now. Probably everyone who moves to town these days thinks it's okay to call himself a Bristolian. But once only those born right on the spot could claim the title.

My great-grandmother was a native. Her parents, too, for all I know. My knowledge of my own genealogy doesn't extend past the rough wooden box that's shoved well under the eaves of 232 Hope Street. My grandmother called it "the Irish trunk."

The Irish trunk held—I assume—blankets or a change of clothes or a crucifix or whatever it is you take when you're running from a famine. Or maybe my ancestors beat it out of Ireland before the potatoes failed; maybe they just had itchy feet. All I'm certain of is that by 1852 there were 300 Irish in Bristol, one of whom or perhaps it was several of whom, had lugged that chest across the Atlantic.

The town they came to was undergoing a slump. It had been rich, thanks to privateering and the slave trade, and it would be middling rich again, once it acquired a rubber mill. But at the moment every other mansion was a boardinghouse, and the poor camped out on the meadows back of town.

Ganny's family, which was large and handsome, married half the town, which is why she had both Catholics and Protestants among her relatives. One of them was a descendant of the man to whom Philip, King of the Wampanoags and son of Massasoit, sold 100 acres near Mount Hope. Mount Hope is a sprawl of mills and swamp and scrub and stagnant ponds and poison ivy on Mount Hope Bay. Philip had his longhouse on Mount Hope, and the quartz throne on which he donned his wampum stole and scarlet cloak overlooks the bay. For centuries Bristol's children risked poison ivy to sit on Philip's throne, but none but Boy Scouts out hiking go there anymore.

In 1676 there was a great battle on Mount Hope; and Philip, who was now trying to oust the settlers from his land, was shot dead. His oracles had told him no Englishman would get him, which was true. Philip's killer was an Indian named Alderman, whose brother he had tomahawked.

Alderman's commander, Benjamin Church, was rewarded with Philip's regalia and Alderman with his hand, which he carried about in a bucket of rum. Four Boston investors acquired the land, laid it out in a grid—four streets by nine—and five years later, at a town meeting, it was christened Bristol. Two hundred years later four Bristol schools were christened after them: the Messrs. Byfield, Walley, Oliver, and Burton.

The first Bristolians attended Congregational services, raised geese and onions, and were legendarily peculiar. But in the mid-eighteenth century a Bristolian named Simeon Potter made a fortune in privateering at about the same time the Church of England sent a missionary. From then on Bristol was more Cavalier than Puritan.

In 1775 the town was bombarded by British warships, and in 1778 British troops burned thirty houses, which is why Bristol's best bear no date earlier than 1784. Lafayette arrived the same year, to set up a line of defense across the Neck, but left when the weather turned chilly. In 1781 George Washington paraded down Hope Street on a carpet of evergreens and pussy willow strewn for the occasion.

Then came the rich years; these were followed by the poor years, and, eventually, the inflation of a modest rubber works owned by one Augustus Bourn into the United States Rubber Company.

By the turn of the century half of Bristol's residents were foreign born, come to work in the rubber mill. Most of them were émigrés from southern Italy, lured—or so the story goes—to Bristol by Terence McCarty, the factory manager and Ganny's uncle. When Terence dropped wages to a dollar a day the employees struck, and he, as cagey as any skinflint Yankee, had handbills touting the Promised Land distributed in Scafati, a town near Salerno.

The Portuguese came too, most of them white, from the Azores. A few of them, *bravas* the color of coffee ice cream, came from Cape Verde. French Canadians arrived, along with a few Jews, a family of Swedes, and a veritable tribe of Syrians.

By the time I began my journey toward Lying-In Hospital the town had Congregationalists, Episcopalians High and Low, Baptists, three varieties of Catholics, Holy Rollers, a flock of Benjamin Church descendants, rich and poor and in between, summer people and locals, teetotalers and drunks and peculiars and—oh Lord!—what *wasn't* there among the 11,000 folk who made up Bristol!

Chapter Three

For many years I have carried in my wallet a photograph of a plump dark-haired man in ice-cream pants standing in front of a tall rosebush and holding a plump dark-haired baby. There is no telling me that I was too young to remember that picture being taken. I am adamant in my recollection of warmth, bees, and the bliss of being in my father's arms.

The rosebush is red, and its tip has been trained to ramble across the wire stretched between it and its twin, a pink rosebush whose tip has also been trained to ramble. Red and pink meet in the middle. Beyond the roses there's a long rectangular plot, nestled next to the sagging blue fence that divides ours from the Tingleys' lawn, planted with phlox and pansies and sweet william; a hydrangea and, behind it, another rectangle, planted with peonies; a flowering quince; a circle of tulips centered by a sundial; a square of more tulips; a grape arbor and, beside it, two pear trees.

Along the back fence are lilacs, hollyhocks, and, in early spring, violets.

Soon my sandbox will be built beside the grape arbor, and my swing hung from its roof. But we aren't yet living at 232 Hope Street, and the arbor still looks as it did when my parents' wedding reception was held in the backyard.

This is my first birthday, and my picture is being taken by our next-door neighbor, Miss Emilie Connery, whose stockings are always wrinkled around her spindled legs and who wears a tailored suit and a felt hat winter and summer. Miss Emilie has a box camera and records such occasions for a small fee. Daughter to Sam and Honey, sister to Miss Aida, who's soprano soloist at St. Michael's Episcopal Church, Miss Emilie is one of the Protestant Connerys.

Another Protestant, Mrs. Emma Rounds, has supplied my birthday cake, angel food with white icing and my name in pink, also for a small fee. Emma is my grandmother's first cousin, one of the Protestant McCartys, and the organist at St. Michael's. Emma is as famous for her angel food cake as Miss Emilie is for her photography. It won't be long before I am famous, too, for being "a good reader."

When, eight months later, my mother, father, and infant sister, Diana, and I move to Ganny and Gampa's house the sidewalk in front is gravel. (Soon the WPA will come and lay cement.) Two blocks further on the gravel peters out and one walks on matted grass. This marks the end of the town proper. Beyond it lies the Ferry, meadows mostly, the estates of the summer people, Narragansett Bay, and, soaring over it, the Mount Hope Bridge, which connects Bristol to Newport. The ferry itself, which the bridge replaced, is long gone. Even so, anyone heading south is heading "down the Ferry."

The harbor is on the other side of Hope Street, and we tell the weather by it. "Red sky at night, sailor's delight," Papa chants when the sun drops blazing into the waves; "Red sky in the morning, sailor take warning," when a gray dawn obscures Poppasquash Point. "Whitecaps today," Mother says some mornings. "It's going to squall."

In a town of beautiful houses, 232 Hope Street is among the ugliest. Not that its builders weren't ambitious. Two flights of steps, one granite, one wood, lead to the glass-paneled front door, and their intersection is marked by a pair of geranium-bearing stone urns. Over the door there's a balcony. To the right of the door there's a two-story bulge of bay windows. Around the corner there's a pair of porches, one on top of the other. Seen head-on the house is narrow, pinched; seen from the side, especially at night when every window is lit, it looks like the *Titanic*. But what supports 232 Hope Street is not the ocean swell but centuries of Indians piled higgledy-piggledy beneath its red-brick cellar. Whenever, barefoot, I prance about the lawn, my toes probe for bones.

The front hall is tall and dark, and at the foot of the curving staircase that leads to our second floor (Ganny, Gampa, and Esther are on the first) is a bronze lady, bare-breasted and barefoot, whose upraised hands hold a lamp. My, but she is lovely, so lovely I trail through the hall dressed in my mother's wedding dress, which has been dyed red, singing holy, wordless songs for her. They are like the vocal exercises I have heard Miss Aida Connery trilling on the Saturday night before the Sunday morning performance, and once my mother says "You're a good girl, Mary Lee, to be singing on Good Friday."

But I am always a good girl and so is Diana. When I ride my tricycle along the cement path next to the windows through which the coal rumbles down the chutes and into the bins, Gampa says "A regular Billy Be-damned." When Diana waddles into the living room dressed in her underpants, Papa announces "The great John L.", and Diana strikes a fighting pose, fists up, fanny out. When we bathe, Gampa and Esther come to watch; when Papa lures us to bed with "Button, button, who's got the button?" they applaud. Only Ganny, too stout and stiff to climb the stairs, stays away. She is in her rocker, reading the *Providence Evening Bulletin* through her magnifying glass.

The *Bulletin* arrives at about four o'clock, hurled to the front steps by a boy on a bicycle, and that means the best part of the day is beginning. In an hour or so, after the five-o'-clock whistle blows, Papa and Esther will come home from the rubber factory, "the shop." The gate to the front steps, one of three in our long green fence, will creak open; Judy, Gampa's cocker spaniel, will bark; and there they'll

AMERICAN GIRL

be, Papa in a three-piece suit and a felt hat, and Esther in a print dress and pumps that show off her pretty legs.

There's always news from the shop and I run up and down the stairs between the messengers, giddy with the bustle they have brought into the house. Downstairs Gampa is in his morris chair smoking his pipe and Esther is saying she's got to rinse out a few things, and Ganny is in the kitchen making supper. Or maybe Esther is upstairs, visiting us, which means that Ganny's going to bang on the riser with a spoon. "Supper's ready, Esther," Di and I chorus, and we race downstairs to see what she's getting. Often we beg to stay.

Downstairs food and upstairs food are different. Downstairs tends toward baked beans, clam chowder, codfish cakes, johnnycake and apple pie. Upstairs is usually a roast, a green vegetable, a yellow vegetable, a starch, and no dessert. Downstairs and upstairs look different, too.

Downstairs, but for the tick of the clock on the fireplace mantel and the drip of the kitchen faucet, is very quiet. It is also very plain. The pictures on the walls of the two parlors are steel engravings and the furniture is hard. Next to the tiled fireplace, which is sealed with a polished brass shield, is a small radio, turned on only for Ganny's daily listen to *Vic and Sade* and Gampa's nightly installment of *Ace 'n' Andy*. "*Amos 'n' Andy*," I tell him, but he won't obey. There are no magazines, but lots of old-fashioned books, thick, with gilt letters on their maroon covers, in a mahogany bookcase.

Esther's room is plain, too, but her closet—Ganny calls it a clothespress—is so big Di and I can walk around it, inspecting her dresses, which are many, and her shoes, which are even more. When we clop into the parlor wearing her high heels, Esther says "Look at those two, would you?" and we clop back, excited, to pick out others.

But the kitchen is the best place downstairs, not at night when it's cold and its corners are dark, but in the morning when it's sunny and Ganny's baking. The kitchen has two stoves, one gas and one coal, and Esther keeps saying "Ma, don't you think it's time you got rid of that old thing?" Ganny won't listen. She puts her bread to rise on top of the coal stove and bakes her beans in its oven. She polishes it weekly with stove blacking and keeps a little poker to stir up the coals, and she claims there's nothing like it for a good, even heat. She has two iceboxes, too, the electric one in the kitchen, and the other in the back entry, which gets a new block of ice twice a week and has a drip pan, which it is my job to empty outside the back door after the iceman leaves. Esther says that while she's at it she ought to throw out that old thing, too, but Ganny says you never know when the lines will come down. That's why she keeps a row of kerosene lamps in the pots-and-pans closet.

Upstairs, Diana and I have our own little maple beds, pushed together because she is forever falling out of hers, our own little blue dining table, and our own little chairs. We also have our own little playroom, off the hall, and our

AMERICAN GIRL

own little silver cups, which make our milk taste thin and steely.

Ganny's bay window has a rocker in it so she can sit and watch the passing scene. Upstairs, though, there's a rope-legged mahogany table on which is a row of books bracketed by leather bookends, a crystal cigarette box monogrammed with Papa's initials, a lamp made from a ginger jar, and a silver-framed portrait of my mother and myself. I, barefoot in white lawn, am on her lap. She, lovely in polka-dotted silk, is smiling like Irene Dunne.

The chairs and couches are fat and squashy, and the dining-room closets crammed with cups and plates and platters. Mother doesn't like to entertain, but people say she sets a beautiful table, and Papa, who does like to entertain, has a glass for every kind of cocktail. "Have a snort?" he asks when somebody drops in after church, and gets out the sugar cubes, the Angostura bitters, and the bourbon. His old-fashioneds are famous, he boasts, for miles around.

My mother calls her parlors living rooms, and fusses because we are impossible. "You will put me in the nut-house!" she cries. Diana can't keep her feet off the furniture and I can't remember to pick the funny pages up off the floor, and Papa leaves his books lying around. Each of us has a favorite place in which to flop, but my mother can't seem to light anywhere. I look like her, and Diana looks like Papa, but both of us have his brown eyes and his blarney and teeth so crooked they seem to dance. We are also to inherit his passion for reading and in a few years the three of us, without lifting our eyes from our books, will sound a simultaneous "Shhh!" whenever Mother comes into the living room. Sometimes she studies us with puzzled eyes, a saluki among spaniels.

The wallpaper in our bedroom has robins on it, and when we take our nap I pretend they are cheeping us to sleep. Naps are after lunch, after a morning out in all weather. We are always outdoors, in the side yard, and I hate that because I want to be indoors, listening to Ganny talk, or lying on the floor upstairs with the funny pages. But I can't come in, my mother says, until there are roses in my cheeks. So I say to Di again and again, "Diana, do you see any roses yet?" Diana loves to be outdoors, and she is never without roses.

But if Esther or Gampa is with us, I'll stay outdoors forever. On summer mornings when she's home Esther takes us across the street to the water for a dip. Gampa comes, too, so strong a swimmer he can ride us on his back. My mother's afraid of the water and sits on the sea wall crying "Don't go out too far. . . . You're turning blue. . . . You're over your heads. . . . Time to come in now." Papa's not afraid, but he can't swim.

He wants us to learn to swim, though; he wants us to learn to do everything. On winter nights when there's snow on the ground and ice slicking the trees, he takes us to Union Street, which rises in a slow hill to High. Then he stands at its foot, to watch out for the traffic on Hope. When he waves,

American Girl

Di and I go down the hill on short, stubby skis toward the dark harbor. It is so cold, so still, and the only sound is a long *s-l-i-i-i-sh*.

Snow, it seems to snow all the time, and once the harbor freezes in thick yellow curls. The white roses on Ganny's porch snow as well, and dusty purple grapes fall on the seat of our swing. The pears fall, too, and the sand in our sand-box, which is shaded by a green-and-orange striped awning, is warm to bare feet. Papa, not Miss Emilie because this is not a great occasion, takes a picture of Esther and me sitting on the little ledge that runs around it. I am skinny and pretty, and so is she, and I am holding a flower to her nose.

Chapter Four

Whenever I speak of him, even now, my eyes fill and my nose gets pink, and I pray the listener won't notice the sudden thickening of my voice. For years after I came to New York, I would watch little girls standing next to their fathers and staring in toyshop windows, or leaning against their shoulders while the subway careened around the curves. I was jealous of those little girls. I envied them the big hands they were holding and the scratch of the tweed or flannel or raincoat poplin against their cheeks. I might have been one of those little girls. Hadn't my father loved New York? Hadn't he spoken of taking me to the shows some day, and buying me a sherry at the Astor Bar? "Oh God," he used to say, "I love that town."

But Ganny! When I talk about Ganny my mouth curls at its corners, and if my eyes are wet it's because they're apt to get runny when I laugh. I am full of stories about Ganny, like the one about the time she lambasted a telephone answering machine for its rudeness. "Now just you slow down," she said. "Just you mind your manners." When we told her that was a recording she was talking to her face flushed. "Dang thing made a fool out of me!"

Let me see her now, in a starched washdress under an apron that didn't come off unless she had callers. Under the dress there's a pink corset so stiff with stays that, folded, it looks like a venetian blind, a pink rayon vest, drawers, and slip. Her stockings stop just short of her knees, where they are rolled into a knot, but no flesh shows because her skirt stops just short of her ankles. Her shoes are black lace-ups, and if I had a dime for every time I tied them—Ganny cannot bend—I would be a rich young lady.

Ganny's eyes are green and somewhat slanted, and her white hair is coiled into a bun. When she goes to bed she takes out the pins and braids it into a long, loose tail. She has never worn makeup, although she likes what she calls a good strong scent, and her face is as unlined as a child's. She also likes thunderstorms, and when they are brewing goes out to the porch, lets her false teeth drop to her tongue, sticks it out, and dares the lightning with her choppers.

Finished with breakfast, I have trudged downstairs for my first morning call, and walked in on the usual scene. Esther is having a fit because once more Ganny has thrown some of her underwear in the incinerator. "Ma," she is screeching, "that was a brand-new slip."

"How was I to know?" Ganny asks, all innocence. "I thought it was just some old thing you wanted to be rid of, the way you left it lying around on that chair." Esther leaves

for work fuming. Ganny trundles out to the kitchen, order-
ing "that dang hound," Judy, to get out from underfoot as
she goes.

In the kitchen is the jug-eared boy from the next town
she married when she was eighteen and he twenty, the eldest
son of a prosperous grain merchant with a walrus mustache
and his handsome wife, who had a bosom you could rest
plates on. He is eating his breakfast egg, crumbling his toast
into the yolk and waiting for his orders. There is no question
about who rules the roost at 232 Hope Street. It is Ganny.
Gampa does as he is told, Esther mutinies only occasionally,
my mother sticks to her own territory—painting tole, cro-
cheting bedspreads, and arranging flowers—and Papa,
though he calls Gampa "Tom," addresses his mother-in-
law as "Mrs. Lonergan." I, to whom she is as inevitable as
sunrise and sunset, shadow her from morning till night
while she makes beds, bakes bread, beats carpets. Short,
stout, Ganny is strong as a navvy.

Labor ceases after the luncheon dishes are washed and
draining by the side of the sink and the day is settled into
somnolence. Afternoons are for strolls—to Eisenstadt's Dry
Goods or the five-and-ten or the foot of Union Street, which
has a fine view of the harbor—and for callers.

The callers are Miss Munro, a small, thin woman with
violet eyes and skin like wrinkled linen, who lives next door;
Mrs. Horton, who wears big hats and has a deep, dark voice
that keeps telling me not to be sassy; and Mame Lannon,
a walleyed widow whose only child is dead. There is a fourth

caller, Hope, but she stays only long enough to give Ganny a small, stitched packet. Hope is the local numbers runner, and secretary of the D.A.R.

Ganny has gambler's blood in her, thanks to her scamp of a father, who went out West and stayed for years, leaving behind two daughters, a son and a wife, the former Bridget McCarty, who died at twenty-eight. "I never liked him," Ganny says, as coolly as if she were dismissing vegetables, which she also doesn't like. When he finally came back East, to three motherless children who'd been passed from hand to hand among their aunts and uncles, he bought a little farm in Massachusetts. "But I never visited," Ganny says. "I wouldn't have given him the sweat off an ice pitcher."

My grandmother loves bingo, the numbers, and, above all, the horses. Every morning she takes the *Boston Daily Record* to her sitting room just off the second parlor, plumps herself into a rocker, and scans the racing pages through her magnifying glass until she finds the horse that owes her money. Then, rocking back and forth to gain momentum, she propels herself from the chair and calls her bookie, a cousin who runs a small variety store. "George," she whispers, "you know who this is. Put fifty cents on Jackie's Girl for me in the fifth." Ganny never gives her name. Maybe the police are listening, she says, and she'll end up in the hoosegow.

When the callers arrive, I lie on the rug pretending to look at the pictures in the big maroon books but of course I am eavesdropping. "Little pitchers have big ears," Mrs.

Horton warns the ladies. But then they forget that I am there and rumble into talk.

The best talker is Mame Lannon, who lives on the very edge of mortality. With no family of her own left to bury Mame likes to help bury everybody else's. While the family is at the funeral she is the neighbor who stays behind to sweep the floor clean of the flowers knocked off the wreaths the undertaker's men have taken to the grave, and put the furniture back into place, and set out the ham and the macaroni salad and the cakes in the dining room and tell the returning mourners of how the deceased had given a little cough, or a little sigh, and just turned his head to the wallpaper. When, still a baby, I tried to get out of Ganny's kitchen and into the parlor where her younger sister, Annie, lay, sunk into the satin of a casket from the Protestant funeral parlor and flanked by guardian gladioli, it was Mame who blocked the door. (Bristol has four funeral parlors, one for the Italians, one for the Portuguese, one for the Irish and assorted converts, and one, Wilbur's by name, for Protestants. My family, by virtue of long residence, become Instant Yankees on dying and are buried by Wilbur's.)

I like these tales of illness and madness and death—there is no small talk in my grandmother's parlor—but I like even more the afternoons when there are no strolls and no callers and Ganny is sitting in the bay window, paring apples and hemming sheets. "Tell me a story," I beg. But not a made-up story. Made-up stories are not for me, and besides, Ganny doesn't know any.

AMERICAN GIRL

Once she told me of Cromwell's siege of Ireland, an eyewitness account as I recall, and surely those were not the words of her father's Canadian ancestors. No, they came straight from the bog, through generations cursed with big, blue, distant eyes—harbingers, according to McCarty legend, of an early death. Mostly, though, she speaks of Bristol, of the massacred Indians and the cranky old Yanks and the ships that once filled the harbor, and of how the Bridies and Nellies and Maggies, servants all of them, sent back to Ireland pictures of a mansion called Linden Place and claimed it for their own. She speaks of Swamp Yankees, who are what the South calls Rednecks, and Black Yankees, who are religious bigots, and of how she wouldn't give either of them house room. Gleefully, she tells the tale of how an uncle of hers chased a Black Yankee named Simmons up a tree, and how that old man Simmons never dared plague him again.

Most of all, she speaks of Bristolians, of the people passing by the bay window and the people buried in the desk, memorialized by sepia photographs on deeper sepia cardboard. To me, the latter—the girls in white lawn and the babies in plaid dresses and the men in shapeless suits and round-crowned hats—are all dead, whether they are or not, and I mourn them as deeply as I do the child who is really gone. On the other hand, they are all alive as well, because when you live in a house that has been a home to so many you always see more people than there are in the room.

Aunt Margaret's doll, wearing my christening dress,

stares from a small chair in Ganny's bedroom. The book she won in fifth grade, a satin-bound copy of the poems of Thomas Moore whose flyleaf reads "To Margaret Lonergan, for Excellence in Spelling," is in Ganny's bureau, and her big, blue, distant eyes watch her survivors from a gilt-framed photograph in Ganny's sitting room. The German shepherd who kept her company during the long nights when, for her health, she slept alone in a tent in the backyard, is buried near the rosebushes. Margaret, the second of Ganny's four children, died when she was eleven. Of pneumonia, Ganny says, but she is lying. She died of tuberculosis, caught from Aunt Annie's husband, and Ganny cannot bear to say the word. Nor can Mame Lannon and Mrs. Horton and Miss Munro. Often I hear them whispering about someone who's "gone up to Saranac" and am puzzled. What and where is Saranac?

"Margaret used to play up to Annie's all the time—oh, they were crazy about Margaret—and Frank was supposed to be over his pneumonia. But she got so thin and so tired, and the doctors around here didn't seem to know anything. So I took her to Providence, and when the doctor came out of the examining room he had tears in his eyes. 'Mrs. Lonergan,' he said, 'if only you had brought her sooner.' "

"You're a good-looking girl, Mary Lee," Ralph Kinder, the florist, said one day when I was sitting on his counter listening to him and Gampa talk about the wreath-and-bouquet count at a big Bristol funeral, "but you're not a patch on your mother. And your mother's not a patch on what her sister Margaret was."

"When your Aunt Margaret was sick," Mame Lannon told me, "young Hezzie Church brought her a little plant. And when she died"—she paused, and fixed me with her round fish-eyes—"the plant died."

All the good ones are dead—Mame Lannon says it's the finest blooms that are nipped in the bud—and their survivors aren't half of what they would have been. Here's Lawrence A., for instance, come to rake Miss Munro's yard. He is very tall and somehow loose, and his face looks like someone went over it with an eraser. Lawrence, who is backward, had a normal twin brother, "but when they were only a few months old he died and his mother was left with Lawrence." Ganny sighs, and together we contemplate God's vagaries.

Here's Mr. C., whose mother jumped off a roof with his baby brother in her arms. Now they're nestled in one coffin up to North Burial Ground, and the air is sweet above their tombstone.

Here's Aunt Annie Clark, the last of Ganny's McCarty aunts and uncles, and the oldest woman in Bristol. Aunt Annie had a sister, Winifred, who married an architect with a famous New England name and went to live with him in Boston. She died young. "Of what, Ganny?" I ask. "Of Boston," she replies.

Here's Ganny's cousin, invisible except to us, in a long

gingham dress and high-topped shoes. When she played the game that children played at birthday parties—whoever pulled out the lump of dirt buried in a box of sand would be the first to die—it was her hand that closed about the damp intruder. She had the McCarty eyes.

Down Hope Street they march, the quick and the dead, and we see the one as clearly as we see the other. Swee' Walla Bullock, the thick-tongued seller of spring water; Indians in single file; the old lady who was poisoned by her relatives; onion farmers and clam diggers; Harold S., whose father spread the Turkey carpet with papers before he put a bullet in his head; Ganny's grandmother, who smoked a pipe; and the demented children of women who, embarrassed by pregnancy, pulled their stays too tight. Meanwhile shadows are eating up the corners of the room, and Nora Bayes is wailing "You left me like a broken da-ha-hahl" on the old wind-up Victrola.

"What are you two doing sitting in the dark?" My mother's in the room, pulling the chain on the table lamp. It's time to fill Judy's bowl, time for *Jack Armstrong, The All-American Boy*, time for Diana to come in from the yard and for Papa and Esther to come from the shop and for Gampa to come down the street from Ralph Kinder's, where he's been chewing the fat all afternoon. Banging the doors, calling out, running up and down the stairs, they'll rouse the house out of the past and into the present. But they are here too late for me. I have come down with the Bristol Complaint.

AMERICAN GIRL

People who have the Bristol Complaint can never leave town. The elm trees snag them. So does the harbor and the wild roses and the history. Some people say the Vikings were here: there's a rock with funny letters on it at Mount Hope, near the throne where Philip, King of the Wampanoags, donned his regalia. Bristol isn't far from Plymouth. On Thanksgiving Day we breathe the Pilgrims' wet, gray air.

Ganny has packed my head with stories, so many I can scarcely close the lid. Every chink is taken up with women tumbling from rooftops and youngsters gathered around a sand-filled box and little girls in white lawn coughing out their lungs. I have never really seen Bristol. I have scarcely stepped beyond our long green fence. Never mind. I see it anyway.

Chapter Five

The first time I saw Diana she was wedged into the corner of a wing chair, wearing an undershirt, a diaper, and a belly band over her healing umbilicus. Her fair hair was little more than fuzz, and her scalp was an angry red. But, then, all of Diana was an angry red. She was screaming, her mouth wide open over toothless gums. Perhaps I'd pinched her.

Emilie Connery came around the corner and through the gate many times, box camera in hand, to photograph the Cantwell girls. Each picture is a testament to mayhem. Sometimes Diana is in her playpen, still in a diaper and undershirt and still screaming. I am standing alongside, in what look like lounging pajamas, and my eyebrows are in one long, mean line. Later there are photographs of us with our tricycle. In some of them Diana hoists a plump, triumphant leg over the seat and grins for the camera while I glower. In others I lay a proprietary hand on the handlebars and stare insolently into space. Beside me Diana is screaming.

Our parents dressed us alike, in little smocked dresses and little black patent-leather shoes for Sundays and little overalls and little brown oxfords for weekdays. Both of us had Papa's brown eyes so we looked a bit alike, but my hair was dark and her hair was light. This made me mad because it meant that I was the evil Rose Red and she was the good Snow White.

Snow White she was, too, dimpled and plump and amiable. But I had thinned out and was all cheekbones and crooked teeth and knees. Esther said that holding me was like holding a bag of bones, and Mother said I'd get into trouble with those hands of mine one day. They were forever after Diana, poking and pushing and, once, going toward her throat until my mother yelled and yanked me away.

Somehow I must have known that once I had no peers, that for eighteen months I had reigned alone. The only time Diana and I were peaceful, when I wasn't shrieking "She did it, she did it!" or "Not fair!" was in bed, in the dark, when I changed her name to Jane and mine to Marie and we conversed. Of what I can scarcely imagine. But I suppose I said things like "Would you like more ice cream, Jane?" and she answered "That would be very nice, Marie."

Other times I tapped out tunes on the maple headboard of my bed. "Baa, baa, black sheep!" Diana would guess, and "Lazy Mary, will you get up!" I liked her then. Even more I liked not being alone in the dark. I liked the sound of her breathing—she was always asleep before I was—and the companionable creak of the mattress when she tossed and turned.

Diana was a tomboy, tearing her clothes on brambles and suffering scraped knees and playing "Run, sheepie, run" with the Tingley boys until it was too dark to see where anyone was hiding. So it was strange when she started getting the stomachaches, strange because it was I who complained of cramps in my legs and tingles in my fingers and believed that I breathed through a hole in my throat. I could feel it, truly, the cold air going in and out of the invisible puncture; and for several months, until I came up with a new peculiarity, I had my mother believing it too.

But this was Diana who woke up crying and clutching her belly, so the pain had to be real. Papa and Mother started whispering to each other. Then Mother whispered to Ganny and Ganny whispered to Esther, but nobody whispered to Gampa because he couldn't be trusted not to be tearful around Diana, who was his pet and his treasure. Once, when Diana had fallen asleep on the couch, I had watched while he picked her up to put her to bed, and his face was blurry with love.

The doctor who lived up the street bustled into the house often, bringing with him peace and sanity and the reassuring scents of ether and rubbing alcohol, but then he, too, started whispering. Papa, he said, would have to call in somebody from Providence.

The somebody from Providence came down, burly in

his topcoat and exuding bonhomie, and said Diana would have to have her appendix out. She cried, fat tears tumbling down fat cheeks, and none of us, not even I, could bear the sight.

Let Papa or Mother even mention the hospital and how she'd have fun and get presents, and tears would well up in those big brown eyes and spill down the cheeks that always had roses in them. "My stomach doesn't really hurt," she'd sob.

The whispering began again, more terrifying than any shout, and I stalked the house with my ears laid flat against my head. Nobody was safe from my ears: Esther said I could hear the grass growing. "We'll tell her we have to take her to Providence for X-rays," Papa whispered to Mother, "and that she'll just have to stay in the hospital overnight. It's the only way we'll ever get that appendix out."

Diana crowed. Neither of us had ever been to Providence, and now she was getting a ride all by herself. Should I tell her what I had overheard? I should not. But now she, in her innocence, was even more of a Snow White; and I, in my knowledge, was even more of a wicked Rose Red.

It was still light on the evening they left for Providence, and Diana, sitting alone in the back seat, her blond pigtails sticking out from under a brown beanie, peered out the rear window at me, who was standing in the roadway. She waved, trustingly and triumphantly, then turned back, safe and happy, to our parents. The car made a left on Union Street, and she was gone.

Two weeks later Diana was home again, with a wonderful scar on her stomach and a wonderful wormlike souvenir floating in a jar of alcohol. It stood on the table between our twin beds and every day it looked a little worse than it had the day before. Bits and pieces of the worm broke off and the alcohol turned gray and turgid, and every morning I woke up to this disgusting reminder of my necessary crime. But I never begged her to throw it out. Guilt wouldn't let me, guilt and that passion to protect which sooner or later is the curse of the oldest child. Those blond pigtails still recede in the distance, and little wisps of hair still disturb our mother's careful central part.

A few months later I awoke with a neck so stiff I was pinioned to the pillow. My head ached too, so badly it seemed a manacle was crushing my skull. Mother and Papa hovered over my bed, and a doctor hovered with them. I remember astonishment and pleasure—finally, I had an ailment that couldn't be treated with a "Mary Lee, you have too much imagination"—and after that I remember nothing.

When I awoke again I was facing a faraway ceiling strung with bright white lights. Slowly, painfully, I turned my head, still pinioned to a pillow, to the left and saw a young black man, the first black person I'd ever seen, lying only a few inches away. His eyes were closed and I willed him to open them, to tell me where we were, but he kept on sleeping. A few days later, listening to the chatter of the nurses who were making up my bed, I heard that he had died.

We had polio, he and I and all the others who were lying on cots in the corridor of this hospital for contagious diseases. There weren't enough rooms to go around. There weren't enough doctors, either. It was a nervous intern who stuck a syringe into my spine and when, many years later, I had a second spinal tap I was astonished to have the first recalled so vividly. I recognized it instantly: that sense that the very marrow is being sucked out of one's back.

When I woke for the third time, I was alone in a great big room. Sometimes a nurse came in, but no one else. Mother and Papa were confined to the doorway, from which they smiled and wiggled their fingers and held up package after package, each wrapped like a birthday present and bristling with bows.

The manacle loosed its grip, my neck relaxed, and I got to sit up in bed and open my presents. Coloring books and paper dolls and picture books, all of which had to be burned before I left the hospital. They'd be covered with polio germs, the nurses said, so I couldn't take them home. Meanwhile I could have a good time.

I did have a good time. I colored in the books and cut out the paper dolls and called out to the little boys across the hall; and when Papa told me that the Bristol public schools were postponing their opening because of the polio epidemic, happiness had me swelling like a toad. I, Mary Lee Cantwell, had single-handedly stayed the school bells, shut the schoolhouse doors, given the schoolchildren (how grateful they should be to me, to me) another week of summer vacation.

Nor was I ever frightened, not even at night, when the windows seemed sad without curtains and the only light was that which seeped under the door. I could hear the nurses' footfalls as they went up and down the corridor, and once in a while the crackle of a uniform when one of them bent over my bed. Fear came later, when I went home.

I was in my own little bed, my little maple bed, nesting and unnesting the *matryoshka* doll Miss Emilie Connery had sent me, and eavesdropping on Papa and Ralph Kinder out in the living room. I was never one for repeating what I heard, and half the time I forgot it anyway. It's just that I loved voices, and language, and that my ears pricked to whispers.

"When they told me an intern had to do the spinal tap," Papa was saying, "all I could think was 'What if the needle slips? What if he misses?' And when I heard she had polio . . . well, Ralph, to tell you the truth I just sat in that waiting room and cried."

Papa cry? Papa lower that big head of his into his big hands and let his shoulders shake and icicles run from his big Roman nose? If my father could cry, than where was safety? If it was not with him, it wasn't anywhere.

A few minutes later I heard him laugh and say it looked like the sun was over the yardarm, so how about a snort? I breathed easier, and felt the fine hairs on my arms—they had risen like a cat's, I swear—lie flat again.

Except for our journeys to the Jane Brown Hospital (that was my sister's) and the Charles V. Chapin Hospital for Contagious Diseases (that was mine), Diana and I had never been outside the country of the blue-eyed. But oh my God, how far I'd traveled.

Chapter Six

I call it the country of the blue-eyed because of something a friend from New York said during a weekend in Bristol. When she looked around the restaurant to which we'd gone for dinner, the restaurant at which my parents had eaten many a lobster thermidor, she said, "Do you realize we're the only people here with brown eyes?"

She was speaking in metaphor, although what she said was also literally true. She is Jewish and I am an Irish Catholic, however well-hidden my roots, and we will never really be at home with a certain kind of Protestant—Episcopalian, usually, with the careless arrogance that can still bring waiters and salesladies to their knees. But as a little girl I lived in their country, and the drawers of my mother's desk are stuffed with mementos of my stay.

This clipping from *The Bristol Phoenix*, for instance: "Little Miss Nancy Church Mossop, daughter of Mrs. Wal-

AMERICAN GIRL

lace Mossop of this town, was hostess Saturday afternoon
at her Poppasquash home to fifteen of her little friends.
. . . She was the recipient of many lovely gifts, including a
Colonial bouquet which was presented to her in a charming
manner by young Bobby Kinder. The time was pleasantly
spent playing games and enjoying refreshments in the service of which Mrs. Mossop was assisted by the mothers
present." The mothers present (mine was the prettiest) stood
behind their children's chairs, poised to intercept the fall of
the fork, the dribble of the ice cream. A few months later,
at my own birthday party, young Bobby Kinder presented
me with a Colonial bouquet in a charming manner.

There's a rosette dangling a faded blue ribbon stamped
with gilt letters that reads "First Prize." It commemorates
my entry—nasturtiums Mother helped me cram into a white
jug—in the junior division of the Bristol Garden Club's
annual show. A ticket stub from my first evening at the
theater, in the Colt Memorial High School auditorium,
when students from the Lee School, which was where the
parents from the country of the blue-eyed sent their children, whirled like dervishes under spinning colored lights.
A snapshot of a group of little girls standing next to the
horse that was the centerpiece of somebody's birthday party.
All of us wore smocked dresses, and might have been cousins to England's little princesses.

I remember Newman's Grocers, where the men wore
white aprons and the butcher a straw hat, and all the eyes

blazed blue. And my mother's bridge afternoons, and the guests forking up meringues buried under strawberries and whipped cream. I remember pale, freckled forearms hung with little purses, and the scent of 4711 cologne, and long, skinny Yankee feet in long, skinny T-strapped shoes. I remember skinny voices too, dry as dust.

Sometimes I heard fatter voices—"Hey, Cheech!" and "Wallyo!" they shouted—coming up from the foot of Union Street on summer afternoons. But I was not to meet their owners for several years yet. My parents, like the people with whom Mother played bridge and Papa played golf, had enrolled their child in the Lee School.

The Lee School, a white clapboard house filigreed with gingerbread, was run by a Mrs. Dunbar and her daughter, Miss Fritzi. They lived on the first floor of the house; the second floor was divided into two classrooms. The big kids sat at desks in the room in front. The little kids sat around tables in the room in back. Almost nobody stayed past fifth grade, although the Dunbars were prepared to soldier on through eighth. Only one student stayed that long, a plain, plump girl with a famous name and a nervous disposition that Ganny blamed on the famous name. Whatever you were, Ganny figured, you were from the beginning. If you were born to a pair of crazy old Yanks you were bound to be a crazy young Yank.

Miss Frizti, whose real name was Frederica, had

bangs and a little crown of braids and was sweet as simple syrup. She smiled, she smiled all the time. She smiled when Billy G. wet his pants and she smiled when Jackie S. threw up, and when she realized that the only way that I could add was by penciling marks on scrap paper and totting them up, she just raised her eyes toward heaven and smiled.

But it was agony to me to be so stupid. The more Miss Frizi tried to show me how to translate the marks into symbols, the more cotton seemed to be stuffing the corners of my head. The cotton seemed even thicker on the nights Papa sat beside me at the desk in the living room, pencil points breaking under his fierce attack. I snuffled and shook and his voice took on a steel edge, and when at last my mother shyly volunteered, the suffering eyes we turned on her were identical.

For several nights she sat at the desk beside this daughter whose eyes had been fixed on her father since the day she was born, and summoned up her old schoolteacher's skills. Sniffling at her left, I bent over a scratch pad watching while her small, shapely hand (a hand that could trace a line of gold leaf as fine as a hair) traced swoops and curlicues. Suddenly they assembled themselves into sense and the cotton fled my head, leaving it as clear and clean as a tide-rinsed seashell. Mother preened, for once sure of herself among these brown-eyed talkative Cantwells, and I knew a triumph second only to that I'd known on the morning I finally succeeded in tying my shoelaces into bows. I could add! I could subtract! But never as easily as I could read.

While the other first-graders—tears in their eyes, spittle wetting their lips—stood beside the tables stuttering out their A's and B's I was busy at the bookcase, diving and dipping in and out of words as freely as a dolphin frisks through water. *Red Feather, The Story of an Indian Boy* was my favorite book: I couldn't get enough of it. The cover was blue and the lettering red, and since my blue beret had a red feather woven into its label, I never ceased to thrill at the coincidence. "Look, Miss Fritzi," I'd command, waving book and beret. She'd smile.

At the Lee School the girls learned to curtsy like duchesses and the boys to bow like dukes, and we all learned "Alouette" and "Sur le pont d'Avignon." In midmorning the boys fell over themselves in the Dunbars' backyard and the girls gathered on the round porch to chatter. We turned our faces to the thin New England sun and sniffed the salty air and watched as Bristol Harbor, just across the street, capered in the light. D.D., who would grow up to be chic, had a big hat that tied under her chin and Ray, who was very tall, had her clothes washed by a laundress, and Nancy, who had red hair, said her mother squeezed oranges for her every morning. I wanted a hat like D.D.'s and long legs and a laundress like Ray's, and wished that my mother would give me orange juice every morning so that I, too, would

AMERICAN GIRL

have hair that flamed like a marigold. Still, D.D. and Ray and Nancy weren't as lucky as I was. They didn't have my father. My father was king of the Lee School's annual Field Day.

Jacket tossed to the ground, shirtsleeves rolled to the elbows of his milk-skinned Irish arms, black hair mussed by the wind, it was end man Leo Cantwell, all 224 pounds of him, who pulled the losing tug-of-war team across the line. It was Leo Cantwell who got slapped on the back, whose face reddened to the cheers and whose mouth split into a smile that was an entertainment in itself. "Who's the handsomest man in the world next to Ronald Colman?" he'd ask when we came home.

"You are!" Di and I would shout.

"Now," he'd say as he tucked us into bed, "you're as snug as bugs in a rug."

And so we were, all the time.

There came a chilly winter morning, though, when Miss Fritzi herded us little kids into the room where the big kids sat and lined us up on chairs facing the blackboard. Then Mrs. Dunbar, short and stout in dusty-rose crepe, told us a story.

The story was about how the king of England—I didn't catch his name—had had to give up his throne because he wanted to marry an American named Simpson. This Mrs. Simpson could never be a queen because she'd been divorced. English kings weren't allowed to marry divorced women, nor, Mrs. Dunbar added, could they marry Catholics.

Not marry Catholics! I had never heard of divorce, so that proscription passed right over my head. But hadn't Nancy once pointed out, her blue eyes fixed speculatively on my face, that I was the sole Catholic at the Lee School? Was it possible that I, the best speller and reader in the whole place, was the only girl there ineligible to sit upon the English throne? What else was I *already* ineligible for, I wondered, and felt a cold, wet finger trace my spine.

I had suspected that Catholics came out of the second drawer ever since I had overheard Gampa complaining about a neighbor who'd refused to sell him a small parcel of land adjoining ours for a garage. "I suppose he thought a Catholic had a hell of a nerve," he said in a cold sour voice.

Another time I asked him why the shallow rise that separated the backyard from the front yard had two stone steps inserted in its center. "Because Protestants lived here," he said in the same sour tone, "and they love airs and graces."

Besides, why else was St. Mary's Church way up in the back of town, close to the rubber factory and a string of low, mean houses and dark, dank stores? Up there the air was yellow and stank of rubber, and there was no harbor breeze to take the heat off a summer day.

Sunday morning, gloved and hatted, we would leave

232 Hope Street, turn right at Constitution, left on High, and walk to the corner of Church. There we'd make another right and start the hike across Bristol Common. What little grass had ever grown on the Common had been beaten down by generations of softball players and schoolchildren, and the Fourth of July visits of traveling carnivals. The elms were lofty, so lofty they brushed the sky, but they were few, and in summer there was no shelter from the sun. In winter there was no shelter from the wind that swept across the Common as if it were the tundra.

St. Mary's Church sheered, rawboned Gothic, out of a steep flight of granite steps, with never a leaf to hide its nakedness. Our pew—our p.u., I thought, using the worst word I knew—was next to a stained-glass window of Jesus and a lamb. Two blocks to the south and west of this chilly sepulcher, my Lee School classmates were filing into ivy-covered St. Michael's for another turn on the social round. But I had been sentenced to Purgatory, forbidden to move, forbidden to whisper, eyes nailed to a faraway figure who bowed and whirled and occasionally extended his arms in our direction. On the rare Sundays when we went to High Mass, incense clouded the aisles and pricked my nose. "P.u.," I'd mutter to myself. Everything was p.u. at St. Mary's Church.

Walking home we moved from yellow to blue, from rubber to salt. The funny papers lay ahead; so did leg of lamb, carrots, lima beans, and a baked potato, vanillaice-creamwithchocolatesaucemarshmallowandwetnuts (always asked for in one breath) at Buffington's Drugstore and, after the sun set and the lamps were turned on, *The Shadow* and Jack Benny. Having traversed Purgatory, I was in Heaven.

Church had imposed an orderly start on what otherwise might have been a shapeless day, and I hated shapeless days. Too, in standing, sitting, kneeling, and bowing on command for an hour, I had achieved that sweet smugness that comes from abnegation. On Sunday, trembling to do good and knowing no beggar with whom to share a cloak and no child to carry across a river, I would instead arrange the dining-room chairs with mathematical exactness, and eat my leg of lamb with all the airs and graces of the blackest Protestant.

The soul was like a sheet of paper, and mine was still unsmirched. Once I reached the age of reason, however, it would be crisscrossed with thin lines if my crimes were small, and thick, terrible strokes if they were big. Thin line, venial sin. Thick stroke, mortal sin. All the marks were erased when one partook of the Blessed Sacrament. Those leaving the altar rail with a mouthful of wafer were walking up the aisle with a just-sponged soul.

This, as I understood it, was why I had to begin Religious Instructions at St. Mary's Parochial School, a brown wooden firetrap of a building near the church. I was nearly seven, thus close to the age of reason, and the warranty that was my baptism was running out. Making my First Communion, it looked like, was a way to renew the insurance.

The class in Religious Instructions met once a week, and although I knew the way to St. Mary's School I was afraid to travel so far outside the country of the blue-eyed by myself. So every Tuesday afternoon, after the Lee School let out, I left salt air for rubber stink to lean against a telephone pole outside the Walley School and wait for the 3:30 bell and Ruthie. If the windows were open I could hear the drone of recitations and the teacher's "Now, class, let's turn to page . . ." and sometimes the slap of erasers. Then the bell tolled and out they'd pour, girls from the door to the left, boys from the door to the right, most of them dark and all of them strangers. All but Ruthie, honey-haired, myopic, and my savior.

Ruthie lived on Union Street with her Boston bull terrier, Brownie, her parents, and her appendix, which, like Diana, she kept in a bottle by her bed. (Eventually everone I knew had their appendix in a bottle by their bed, everyone but me, who still worries if the pain—from too much wine, too many shrimp—is on the right.) Our parents weren't friends, they were scarcely acquaintances, but I think my mother had called her mother to ask if Ruthie could be my guide to St. Mary's. I trailed her as trustingly as I would have trailed Leatherstocking, and in a sense I trail her still.

We sat in a tan classroom strung with pictures of the Crown of Thorns, the Light of the World, and the Sacred Heart, holding small tan catechisms and facing an apple-faced nun, mysterious in her floating black, responding in rote:

"Who made the world?"

"God made the world."

"Who is God?"

"God is the creator of heaven and earth and of all things visible and invisible."

Were the nuns bald? Like every child who's ever faced those high calm foreheads, we wondered if they extended to the nape of the neck. What was the nuns' underwear like? Surely they couldn't wear corsets and pink drawers like Ganny. They must wear muslin, and it must scratch. One nun, Sister Edwina, said that she loved Saint Peter most of all the saints because he had sinned. So Ruthie and I also loved Saint Peter best, mostly because we liked Sister Edwina and partly because (as we realized many years thereafter) we were more comfortable with sinners. All the nuns, when asked to explain the inexplicable, answered with a sibilant "But that, my child, is a myssssstery."

On these Tuesday afternoons the questions for which there were no answers, only cloture, mounted in a tall, dusty pile and the air grew thick enough for stirring. When—and oh, God, how the clock stalled in its paces—it was five o'clock and we filed out of the classroom and down the wooden steps I was as frantic as if I'd been sewn into a shroud.

By that hour the Common was almost dark and usually empty, and I would urge Ruthie to a race along the sidewalk that bisected it from northeast to southwest. It puzzled

Ruthie, this wild run across the Common, and sometimes she slid opaque glances in my direction. No matter. Once we were on High Street we were out of the grave, and fresh air was lifting my hair and brushing my cheeks again.

At home I waited for the myssssstery to reveal itself. I hungered for the arrow that would pierce my body and make me a child of Christ. I begged God to appear in our bedroom some night after Diana had drifted off to sleep so I could see Him, and when He didn't I climbed to the attic and prayed to Aunt Margaret. The attic was that much closer to Heaven and surely she, who was bound to be there—if indeed there was a there—would bend her sad blue eyes in my direction and smile.

"Please, dear Jesus, give me a sign," I'd whisper, and finger the rosary I'd stolen from Ganny's bureau drawer, ashamed not just of theft but of ascribing magic to a string of little beads. The attic was very cold and musty, and the old trunks and stripped-down bedsteads looked lonely in the dark. The Irish trunk stood derelict under the eaves, and chamber pots that had held the piddle of people long gone were stacked on a closet floor. A hand-tinted photograph of my mother, taken when she was about two years old and blond as an angel, swung crooked from a nail. I waited. The silence was absolute. There was nothing and no one to be heard up here.

On a Sunday morning in May I made my First Communion, fearful of the absentminded sip of water that would break the fast and of the accidental rip of the teeth that would torture the Host. Esther took my picture in the backyard that afternoon. My veil was drooping, my long white stockings, dependent from my first garter belt, were drooping, and so was I.

Chapter Seven

It is an autumn evening one year later, and Gampa's garden has been put to bed for the winter. I am sitting on a chair in the kitchen, directly under the ceiling light, and a towel is draped about my shoulders. My hair has been drenched with something that smells like kerosene and my mother is parting it into inch-wide sections, then riffling through them with a fine-toothed comb. Every once in a while she says "Gotcha!" and shakes the comb over a wastebasket. Like everyone who has ever shared a classroom with a member of the notorious V——— family, I have cooties.

Obviously I (and Diana, who is next in line for the kitchen chair) am no longer at the Lee School. No louse has ever crossed its threshold. Our parents have taken us out of there and enrolled us in public school. We go quietly, disappointed only that they wouldn't let us skip a grade. Given a mother who used to teach school and a father on the School Committee, we're a year ahead of ourselves. No, they said, you're too young. So here we are at the Walley

School, Di in the second grade, I in the third grade, and both of us with lice.

Papa believes in the public schools as fervently as he believes in the Holy Ghost, the Holy Catholic Church, the Communion of Saints, the Resurrection of the Body and Life Everlasting, amen. Parochial schools will narrow our minds and our prospects. Private schools are all right if they're in Switzerland, which is where the richest man in Bristol sent his children, because there one has all the advantages of Europe. Otherwise they represent the most arrant form of snobbery. Why, when he was a boy in Fall River the daughters of textile tycoons sat side by side with the sons of millhands, and that's the way America's supposed to be. So off we trotted, in eyelet-edged underwear and sashed gingham dresses from Gladding's, Providence's nicest department store, and carrying elaborate plaid schoolbags.

My first day at the Walley set the tone for all the years to follow. Still as timid about leaving the country of the blue-eyed as I had been when I was taking catechism lessons, I tagged after Ruthie. She ushered me through the squirming crowd at the entrance marked "Girls" and through the dreary corridors and up to the big square classroom. But once in my seat—last one in the first row—I was on my own. And the first thing I did was insult the teacher.

I corrected her spelling. "It's not p-s-l-a-m, Miss P———," I said of the word she'd written on the blackboard. "It's p-s-a-l-m. You've spelled it puh-slam." I giggled, thinking she'd see the joke. Miss Fritzi would have. "Don't you be so smart, Mary Lee Cantwell," Miss P——— snapped, and her eyes were a basilisk's.

An hour or so later the music teacher, a barrel of a woman with a chin you could wrap your hand around, bustled into the room. She chalked some notes on the blackboard with short, vicious strokes, then went around the room, asking each student to read aloud those she jabbed at with her pointer. When she got to me I rose from my desk and said "I'm sorry, Mrs. D———, but I haven't been taught how to read music." "I'm sorry, Mrs. D———," she replied in perfect mimicry, "but I haven't been taught how to read music." I sat down, my eyes hot and my stomach melting. Till then I had believed that all rooms would brighten because I entered them. As we walked home after school, Ruthie was silent and her eyes were opaque behind her plastic-rimmed glasses.

For a few weeks I was a novelty. The girls gathered around me at recess and lifted my skirt to see my French pants, which they admired, and touched my hair ribbon, which they said was "so-o-o-o pretty." Years later I saw Gypsy children behave like that, stroking and soothing and cooing like doves while we tourists moved down a Yugoslav street, fearful lest those little brown fingers slip inside our purses. But now I was flattered and showed off a little, and offered my Smith Brothers Cough Drops to the crowd.

Except for Ruthie and a handful of others, my classmates were the children and grandchildren of immigrants, and they lived near the rubber factory. Their grandmothers wore shawls and stumbled over English, if they spoke it at all, and on feast days their fathers, stocky men in dark, shiny suits, bent their backs to wooden platforms from which plaster saints bestowed frozen blessings on the crowd. They and their families had changed the face of Bristol from blue-eyed to brown, from fair-skinned to olive, and their names were slippery and suspect to the northern tongue.

Down on the Yacht Club dock on summer Saturdays a legion of ladies, summer people and Ferry residents in Best & Company shirtdresses, were barking "Well *done!*" as the winning Herreshoff bull's-eye crossed the finish line, while up on the Common men in shirtsleeves were playing boccie. Meanwhile the last Yankees roamed their enclaves—the Neck and the southern ends of Hope and High Streets—the blue veins under their thin skins knotted across their knuckles and their shinbones. Not only were they dying, they were dying out.

Public school, though, was in another country. Give an Italian the eye and he, or she, would give you the finger. And a shove and a fist and, once, a curse. When Papa insisted that a tubercular teacher leave her job for treatment, her relatives telephoned 232 Hope Street and told him they hoped his daughters would die of the same disease.

The novelty wore off, my innocence seemed arrogance which, in a way, I suppose it was, and now the crowd of girls who circled me at recess shouted "show-off!"

and "stuck-up!" and "School Committeeman's daughter!" When I erred and revealed my report card they added "teacher's pet."

The hits that knocked me out of the ring during dodge ball were hard enough to leave a bruise, and I was always the last to be chosen for a team, any team. Often at recess I wet my pants from fear and nervousness, and spent the rest of the day sitting on one haunch so the moisture wouldn't seep through my dress. At night I rinsed out my underwear so my mother wouldn't see it, and during the day I sucked up to my tormentors, and distributed my cough drops with an ever more lavish hand. Once I brought a girl home to play after school, and when she said of the root beer my mother poured her "Oh, I've never had such a big glass before," I felt her well-aimed shiv between my ribs.

To be part of the gang I was willing to strip myself of my gingham dresses and my little red topper, my twenty-five cents a week and my giant box of Crayolas. What I couldn't discard was a home in the country of the blue-eyed, to which most of the kids at the Walley had been only for afternoons at the foot of Union Street, and I seldom made it to the blackboard without feeling the sting of a ruler on the back of my legs. When a girl with a pinched face turned out to be consumptive and became the toast of the school for the week before she left for a sanitarium, I envied her, so much so that every time I brushed my teeth I studied the spit, hoping for the bloody threads that would bring me,

too, the love and admiration of my classmates. Then a new
girl arrived, and for a blessed while nobody paid attention
to me.

She sat for a few tortured months in the back row, her
gray eyes anxious in her pudding face and her fat red hands
knotted around one another. Every morning she traveled
across the harbor on the Prudence Island ferry, and she
reeked of fish and unwashed underwear. When we went
outside at recess she stood alone, isolated by her terrible
odor, while the V——— family, monuments to impetigo
and perpetually painted with gentian violet, swarmed
the Common, little boys fought to see little girls' underpants, and I, in the majority for once and desperate to remain
there, smiled the smile of Uriah Heep and turned away
my face.

The teachers at the Walley, like most of those in town,
were Irish and Italian and Yankee spinsters, graduates of
the Rhode Island Normal School. The only one (besides
Miss P———) who sticks in my mind is the one who got
married, and that only because everybody stared at her when
she came back from her honeymoon, to see if she walked
differently. Rumor had it that she would, though why wasn't
specified, and I thought I detected a certain looseness
through the thighs.

Every morning we pledged allegiance " 'a the flag of
the United States of America," sat down, bowed our heads,
and said the Lord's Prayer. How it ended depended on

whether the teacher was a Catholic or a Protestant. If she was the former her mouth snapped shut after "and deliver us from evil, amen," while the few Protestants among us continued with a loud and confident "For thine is the kingdom and the power and the glory. . . ." If the teacher was a Protestant her voice was loudest of all.

What did I learn, aside from two into six goes three and mis-sis-sippi spells Mississippi and how to convert my private-school printing into Palmer Method script? I learned how democracy works. Like this: Different-sized pegs are hammered into holes until they are all exactly the same height.

"Fair's fair, democracy wins," the kids yelled about everything from choosing sides for softball to class projects. So did Miss P———. Democracy lost, for instance, the day Papa gave me a dime-store bridge to span the pocket-mirror pond that was the centerpiece of my Japanese garden. (We were making pie-tin landscapes.) "That's not fair to the others, Mary Lee," she said, "because not everybody's got a father who can afford to buy them bridges." I blushed, ashamed of myself and my garden and even of my father, who was so eager to help his children and so ignorant of the rules. When the teacher asked which of us wanted to bring home notices of the PTA meetings, I waved my hand and said I was sure my parents would want them. But my parents never went to the PTA meetings; I doubt anybody's parents went to the PTA meetings. Our world of dusty erasers and basement toilets and desks and chairs bolted to the floor was ours alone.

By early afternoon the sun slammed the windowpanes and the exhalations from forty squirming bodies slammed the ceiling. One of the big boys was summoned to let in fresh air with the long pole kept in the corner. Up he stretched, his shirttail going up with him, making pass after pass at the hole in the top of the window. Finally, the pole's metal hook caught, he tugged, the windows shimmied down an inch or so and in rushed the scent of rubber and dust and trampled grass. We lifted our noses, some of them blocked with boogers. We trembled, like horses in full whinny.

One morning during recess a wind came up and blew the dirt about as if it were tumbleweed. The grit freckled my bare legs, and the sky was a sick yellow. Some of the teachers, Diana's among them, sent their classes home. Miss P——— delayed—she thought the wind would die—and by the time she realized it would not, trees were falling without a whisper. I, stranded alone on High Street among toppled elms and hissing electric lines and a sound like a cow lowing, was more interested than scared. Being caught outdoors in a hurricane struck me as part and parcel of being in the third grade at the Walley School.

Ruthie, my mother said, had "personality." Her parents came from out of town, which was enough to make her a foreigner in Bristol; that her father was a Swedish Lutheran and her mother a Polish Catholic only compounded her otherness. But I think it was that otherness, and the attendant wariness, that allowed her to navigate the public schools so successfully. Ruthie, as I could see by the crowd of kids that trailed her out the schoolhouse door, was a political genius. With Ruthie one was protected. Hanging around her was a lot like hanging a scapular around your neck.

After the Walley let out for the day we sometimes stayed up on the Common, playing tag or marbles—squatting in the dust and aiming aggies at the hole dug by twisting one's heel into the dry soil—until the sun sank and the wind chilled and the lights came on in the little High Street houses. Other days we scuffled through the leaves that carpeted Wood Street, all the way down to Tanyard Lane, where skunk cabbage perfumed the air in spring and the tree growing out of the roof of a crypt in an old family graveyard—"Its roots are in his skull," we'd shriek—made us shiver. There were no houses down here, only tall grasses and soughing trees and the occasional cow strayed from the meadows down the Ferry, and our eyes were eager for Indians, miraculously resurrected and padding noiselessly across the swampy ground.

More often, though, I trusted to my own company, mine and Ganny's, to get me through the hours till Papa and Esther came home with the news from the shop. Like Judy,

I was forever underfoot. "You might as well come up street to the Bluebird Shoppe," or "I suppose you want me to take you to the five-and-ten," Ganny would sigh, and trundle into her bedroom for her hat.

Ganny's hats were brimmed, bowed, and often fruited, sat square on her head and announced she was going places. The only time she went out without one was when she was just crossing the street to look at the harbor. Then her white hair escaped its pins and flew around her face and turned her into a short, plump maenad. Whenever, now, I hear the term "Wild Irish," I think of my grandmother at the foot of Union Street, the water dancing and her hair streaming and her green eyes glinting like beach glass.

The Bluebird Shoppe was owned by Miss Norah Sullivan, a tall, stout, sternly buttressed women who was privy to every female bump and bulge in our part of town. Entering the Bluebird's deep amber gloom was like entering a church. Voices were as hushed as they were at St. Mary's, the customers leaning toward Miss Sullivan much as they would toward the grille of a confessional and murmuring into her bottomless ears. If I concentrated I could catch a word or two—"garment . . . support . . . bust"—and once, from Ganny, a sibilant, sinister "truss."

Silently the long thin boxes slid in and out of the shelves, and the tissue paper rustled discreetly when it opened to reveal corsets whose laces were longer than those that tied my shoes and garters that dangled obscenely when

AMERICAN GIRL

Miss Sullivan pulled the "garment" out of its virginal wrap. Together Ganny and Miss Sullivan whispered while Ganny ran a small, fat hand over her stomach and I, half-thrilled, half-mortified, shivered at what it meant to be female. Ganny disappeared behind a curtain. Miss Sullivan followed.

"Watch out for my hairpins." Miss Sullivan was pulling Ganny's dress over her head. "I could take it a little tighter." Miss Sullivan was lacing. "Here, just under the bust, it . . ." I felt sick.

I always took a deep breath when we left the Bluebird, driving out the sweetness of dusting powder and sachet with the punch of salt and privet. "Now," I'd command, "the five-and-ten," and off we'd go, slowly because of Ganny's rheumatism, to the true up street. "Anybody want anything from up street?" the grownups said whenever they left the house for the drugstore or the five-and-ten, and my mind would reel with possibilities.

At the five-and-ten, which smelled of the Spanish peanuts roasting in the big machine by the entrance, I studied the paper dolls and Ganny poked among the spectacles, looking for something that might replace her magnifying glass, and there one day she lost her underpants. The elastic gave way; they puddled, pink and voluminous, to the floor; she scooped them up with the end of her rubber-tipped cane and walked on, imperturbable. "No sense in being embarrassed," she said, seeing the skin around my eyes turn red, and stuck the underpants in her handbag.

From the five-and-ten, where we seldom bought any-thing and marveled over everything, we ambled down to Eisenstadt's Dry Goods, Ganny how-doing from side to side as we went. While she bought muslin for her nightgowns —V-necked, long-sleeved, and plain as sheets—I wandered the aisles, giddy among the bolts of fabric and tumbles of yarn and the sharp, clean scent of sizing. Then, past Buf-fington's and the jewelry store and the Y.M.C.A. and Alger's Newsstand and the ever-open, beer-haunted door of the Belvedere Hotel, we strolled toward home.

After Constitution Street the salt breeze got stronger and the trees moved with it. In the distance the bay windows of 232 Hope Street gleamed like a lighthouse lantern, and behind them Gampa watched as his short, stout Mag, lean-ing on her cane, came slowly into view. Tonight Ganny might take me to bingo up over G.A.R. Hall, and tomorrow she might take me up to Milk Street and let me watch while Miss Brelsford measures her for her nightgowns, and the next day she might let me go with her while she calls on Mrs. Horton, and never will she let me know that she knows that nobody at school likes me.

Instead she will infuse me with her delight in the or-dinary. The one time I played bingo as an adult, on a Cunard liner crossing the Atlantic, my fingers were joyful on the old familiar markers. The day I wriggled into my first girdle and felt the garters bounce against my thighs I was returned to the Bluebird Shoppe and possessed of all its delicious, illicit, secretive femaleness. And whenever I smell starch or Spanish peanuts my veins fill with something that fizzes like ginger ale. Up, up, up it goes, to the top of my head, which has never worn, and probably never will wear, a bowed, brimmed, and fruited hat.

Chapter Eight

If only my memory were more merciful. But let me climb the steps to 232 Hope Street and I remember the day a boy who was inarticulate with rage and perhaps love threw a stone at my receding back and broke one of the door's engraved glass panels. The glass that replaced it was frosted, with no curlicues, and stares at me now, ugly as a cataract.

Let me go down to the foot of Church Street to buy lobsters off the wharf, and I see a muscular girl named Teresa wrestling me to the ground, her dress riding up over her underwear and her socks sliding ever deeper into her shoes while her seconds, a gang from the back of town, cheer her on. I can see myself, too, struggling to stay upright and conspicuously short of adrenaline. This, I was thinking, is *dumb*.

Let me run a hand along the back of my head and my fingers probe for a scar that disappeared decades ago: souvenir of the day that Ruthie and I found a lost puppy.

It was shivering near the entranceway to Miss Hill's

house. Miss Hill was principal of the Byfield School, where we were now fourth-graders, and traveled its halls like a miniature tank. We were very respectful of Miss Hill. To be otherwise was to sit, silent and seemingly forgotten, on the straight chair outside her office door until she looked up from her desk and said the punishment period was over and don't you ever do it again.

I suspect it was to get into her good graces, to show ourselves good citizens, that Ruthie and I thought of asking Miss Hill, and not our mothers, what we should do about the puppy. But as we stood hesitating over which of us should ring her bell, a boy who lived near the rubber factory, the same boy who had thrown the stone that broke the glass panel in the front door, came along and said, "Give it to me."

"Why should I?"

"Because I said," he answered, and tried to pull the puppy from my arms. When I hung on to it, he pushed down on the cement sidewalk, splitting my scalp. The blood pooled around my head and he, frightened, ran for home. For weeks thereafter my skull was swathed in gauze and adhesive tape and I wore my bandages as arrogantly as if I were sporting the stigmata.

Even so, the boy had scared me. I thought he was crazy then and I think he is crazy now, and on the rare times when I see him—an unremarkable adult with a head that has lost its hair and a chest that had slid into his stomach—I pass without speaking. I can take care of myself, but the skinny, chattering girl I was could not, and I'm still touchy on her behalf.

There are others in Bristol, housewives and plumbers and electricians now, whom I might pass without speaking if I were certain that they had been among the crowd that followed me home from school one winter afternoon. But I'm not certain, because my eyes were fixed on the feet, shod in oxblood-colored cordovan with bright yellow laces, that were slowly and stubbornly taking me home.

My fifth-grade teacher at the Reynolds School, not realizing how unpolitic her choice, had chosen me as my home room's entrant in the school's annual talent show. In truth I had little talent, only a thin soprano that reached a lot of perilous notes. But I thought it was wonderful to be able to sing so high, and, turning the playroom into my rehearsal studio, practiced my entry every day. "Now 'neath the silver moon," I piped, and thrilled to my baroque "Sa-a-a-nta Lu-ci-i-a, Santa Lu-cia!"

On the night of the talent show we, as usual, left the house in a body: Ganny and Gampa walking very slowly up front, followed by Papa, Mother, and Esther, with Diana and me bringing up the rear. Into the Reynolds Auditorium we walked, a familiar place because it was the site of Bristol's Town Meetings, and my family solemnly took their places on the folding chairs. I joined the others onstage and, when the lights went down, strained to see them in the dark, sitting breathless lest I forgot the words.

AMERICAN GIRL

The principal called my name. I stepped forward and stared blindly at the invisible audience. And I sang it! I sang "Santa Lucia" all the way through, without forgetting a word, and waited for the applause. But there was none, because when I stopped the piano went on. The accompanist was expecting me to sing the second verse. I didn't know it.

Later on I wished I'd pretended to faint, but I doubt it would have helped. If the bandages I'd worn around my head in fourth grade hadn't brought me love, lying supposedly unconscious on the stage of the Reynolds auditorium wouldn't bring it either. Instead I said to the accompanist, a friend of my mother's, "Mrs. Sturdevent, I didn't learn the second verse."

"Well, then, Mary Lee," she said, "why don't you sing the first verse over again?" So I did.

I was sitting with the residents of 232 Hope Street, all of them sad and quiet, when the judges announced that Mary Lee Cantwell had won first prize, a subscription to *American Girl* magazine, for her homeroom. Ruthie, who was sitting in the row in back of us, leaned over. "I think you'd better walk to school with me tomorrow," she whispered.

For now, though, there was the walk home along the sleeping streets and Gampa saying "Mary Lee, you did fine," and Papa saying "It's okay, Lulubelle. All famous actresses forget their lines once in a while," and Diana on the verge of tears because it is embarrassing to be my sister.

MARY CANTWELL

And I? I was locked in a misery that has lasted me all my life. Let me hear "Santa Lucia"—and it seems to me I hear it all the time—and I am, for a moment, humiliated.

The next morning Ruthie was waiting for me at the corner of Constitution Street. We didn't speak while we trudged along High Street, and my back was damp with cold sweat. No one would come after me while I was with her, they wouldn't dare, but what would happen at lunchtime? Ruthie carried sandwiches to school because her mother was a nurse at the rubber factory, and I would have to go home alone.

At noon the mob settled quietly into place behind me, like birds settling on a telephone wire. At first they were silent, until somebody shouted "School committeeman's daughter!" Then all of them took it up. "School committeeman's daughter! School committeeman's daughter!"

My eyes stayed on my shoes, my shoes and the passing squares of pavement that told me that slowly, slowly I was nearing Constitution Street. Once I got there I would be entering the country of the blue-eyed, and the mob would stop at the border.

Constitution Street was less than a block away when a stone hit my arm, Another hit my back, and a third my leg and then they came in torrents, stones and pebbles and handfuls of dirt. On I plodded, turning left and up the steps of a small grocery store. "Mr. McCaw," I said to the owner, "could you please call my house?"

"Tom," he said when Gampa answered, "I think you'd better come up here and get Mary Lee."

When Gampa arrived, I was standing on the little porch of McCaw's Grocery and the mob was standing a few yards away, watching me with quick, curious eyes. Gampa didn't look at them, nor did he say a word to me. He simply extended his long, liver-spotted hand and escorted his grandchild across Constitution Street. I was over the border now, and safe.

Chapter Nine

Never mind. I had friends. Slowly, very slowly, we found
one another. We recognized our tribal markings. We heard
them in our speech—"ahsk" instead of "ox," for instance
—and we spotted them in the the long white cards with the
black printing on top that marked our membership in the
Rogers Free Library. We all had mothers who wouldn't let
us out of the house without a clean handkerchief in our
schoolbags, and our shoes—sober oxfords—came from the
same sober Providence shoe store. Four of us took piano
lessons and I took watercolor lessons and except for Jeanne,
who had three siblings and countless aunts, we came from
small families. Ruthie, of course, and Jeanne, Joanie, Anne,
and I. We didn't so much meet as coalesce, and we stayed
together until the night we graduated from Colt Memorial
High School. Two of us were Catholic and two of us were
Protestant and one of us was half and half, and for all of
us our strongest spiritual bond was with the Girl Scouts.

AMERICAN GIRL

The Columbines met as often in winter and spring as they did in autumn, but in my mind the afternoons are always golden and the leaves are always turning as we Scouts file in the door of the Burton School and hang our coats on its old hooks.

The Burton, which was up on High Street, smelled of chalk and oiled floors and we smelled of wool and jujubes. The room (there were only two) in which we met to master the skills that earned us merit badges was bare and yellow in the western sun, and its radiators were forever thunking. I loved it there, the warmth and the coziness and the going to the bathroom in pairs, one of us pretending nonchalance while the other piddled into the toilet. We were fascinated by our bodies, and pretended to be casual about them by peeing in company, just as one day we would broadcast our menstrual periods. "Oh," we'd moan in years to come, "I'm like the Mississippi at flood tide."

We pretended to be casual about boys' bodies too, but a purloined copy of *The Boy Scout Handbook* was continually passing from hand to hand and falling open, automatically, to the chapter titled "Containment." It was erotic, unbearably so, with its talk about "nocturnal emissions" and the wisdom of sitting in a cold hip bath for fifteen minutes before bedtime and of seeking advice from "wise, clean, strong men." Powerful, too. "Keep control of yourself in sex matters," the handbook thundered. "It's important for your life, your happiness, your efficiency, and the whole human race." No wonder we never saw the boys of Troop Five, our brother troop, on parade without thinking of their silent, superior struggle and of the volcanoes concealed by their rolled-up (to signify they were veterans of Camp Yawgoog) khaki shorts.

About those skills we mastered: We tied knots, I know that, and one night we went to the home of the wife of the local optometrist for a lesson in spaghetti sauce and washing one's hands between bathroom and kitchen. For this exercise we were awarded the hostess badge. I had other badges too, plastering the left sleeve of my silvery-green uniform, but for what I no longer remember. Fire-making probably, and tree identification for sure. I can still tell an elm from an oak, and a birch from a maple.

I can recall the marching, though, around and around the patch of grass in front of the Burton, practicing for the Memorial and Armistice Day parades. Once, as I was counting a *sotto voce* "one-two, one-two," a fly flew in my mouth and was promptly swallowed. "I'm not surprised," my mother said. "Your mouth is always hanging open." She said I talked too much. Papa said I had the gift of the gab.

But all that practicing paid off. When we marched up Hope Street on parade mornings, I with the end of the staff that flew the Girl Scout flag nestled next to my belly button, we were a sight. The Goldenrods and the Marigolds weren't in it with us. When we passed 232 Hope Street, stepping smartly, my family clapped and Gampa raised his hat—felt

on Armistice Day, straw on Memorial—for the Stars and
Stripes. When we stood near the flag-markered graves in
North Burial Ground and the bugler played "Taps," I threw
back my shoulders and presented a brave face to the west.
And when, on the evening of Armistice Day, Ruthie and I
walked along High Street after the service at the Train of
Artillery Hall, through the rustling trees and the dry leaves
and the damp air, after the speeches and "My Buddy" and
"There's a Long, Long Trail a-Winding," we were too blissfully sorrowful to speak. How lovely it was to feel the tears
flowing down your cheeks and know that no adult could tell
you to stop that sniffling, because you were weeping in a
good cause.

Every spring I roamed the neighborhood, pad in hand,
taking orders for Girl Scout cookies. A talker but shy, I never
knocked on a stranger's door. Instead I called on Mrs. Connery, mother to Miss Aida and Miss Emilie, and Mrs. Tingley, who lived on the other side of the blue fence, and
Ganny's friend Miss Munro, nosing around their back entries and sniffing at the smells from kitchens other than my
own. On the day the cookies arrived at the Burton School I
trotted out of 232 Hope Street after supper, my arms hooked
around the boxes, feeling as if I were digging my heels into
Bristol, that I was as much a part of its fabric as the iceman or the coalman. "Hope you enjoy them!" I'd say to
Mrs. Connery, Mrs. Tingley, and Miss Munro, all of them
flushed from cooking and fishing in their change purses. I

sounded exactly like the man on the Arnold's Bakery truck.

Mrs. Connery, Mrs. Tingley, Miss Munro, Miss Aida, and Miss Emilie were looking out their windows the night I walked up Union Street for the Girl Scout dance. I know this not because I saw their faces or the twitch of their curtains but because in Bristol watching somebody leave the house for her first dance and the Junior Prom and her high school graduation was a way of telling time.

I had thought long and hard about what to wear, and finally settled on a yellow cotton blouse, a teal-blue wool skirt with a brown leather belt, beige knee socks and brown oxfords. What I hadn't thought about was not knowing how to dance. Perhaps I believed it would just come to me, or that simply being there, under a ceiling crisscrossed with crepe paper and surrounded by Pennsylvania Six Five Oh Oh Oh would be enough. Perhaps it would have been, too, except that Albert, Joanie's brother and a member of Troop Five, led me away from the rest of the Columbines and onto the floor. "No, Mary Lee," he said when I extended my right arm toward his shoulder. "Put your left hand on my shoulder and let me hold the other one." I did as I was told and then, staring intently at my feet, tried to make them follow his. They did!

Tall, blond, three or four years older than I, Albert never shared a dance, or even a dance floor, with me again. Still, he was the first male whose movements I had ever tried to mirror: and those slow, flat-footed steps of mine were, I realize now, as irrevocable as those with which, a baby, I had tumbled into my parents' waiting arms.

Usually I grabbed every opportunity to put on my Girl Scout uniform and proclaim to the world my membership in a club, but not on the Fourth of July. Bristol's parade was the oldest in the country, and maybe the biggest, and I wouldn't have dreamed of marching in it. Miss the floats, the governor of Rhode Island, the drum-and-bugle corps from all over New England, the Fourth of July Committee with their ice-cream pants, boutonnières, and malacca canes, the antique cars and the fire engines and the servicemen from Newport and Jamestown and points north? Miss the balloon men and the eggnog Papa put in the punch bowl in the front hall and the thrill when some of the marchers—the governor, even—flourished their hats to his applause? They knew him! Leo Cantwell, member of the Bristol School Committee and defeated candidate for the Bristol Town Council. But only because it was a bad year for the Democrats.

Early in the morning when the sky is still gray we can hear the dull boom of the Fourth of July cannon. "Get up," my mother pleads. "Get up, get up, get up." Time to get out the old blankets and the folding chairs and spread them over the banking in front of 232 Hope Street because if you don't make it clear that this strip of grass is yours, all yours, people from out of town will come and park their carcasses right in front of you.

The Barrington crowd, friends of Papa and Mother, are up early, too, because if they aren't, strangers will take their parking places. Barrington is about ten miles from Bristol, a pretty place, more suburb than town, with the highest number of blonds per capita in Rhode Island. The Barrington crowd plays a lot of golf.

"We're going to have an army in here," my mother says, shooing Di and me out of the kitchen, out of the bathroom, out of the house. "Don't dirty those towels, don't use those glasses, put those books away this minute." Downstairs Papa is mixing the eggnog in Ganny's big punch bowl. "My theory," he says as he dribbles in the brandy, "is that everyone will have gotten here too early to have had breakfast. And here we have eggs and cream. . . ."

Esther, still buzzing from the night before the Fourth at the Belvedere—all Bristol meets there on the evening of July 3 to hoist a few—and dressed in red, white, and blue, is knocking ice cubes out of a tray. It's only nine o'clock in the morning, mind you, but she, like a lot of Bristolians, will spend the day with a glass in her hand. Gampa, having crawled out the window in the playroom, is on the balcony over the front door hanging out the American flag. Judy, her little backside wriggling, is barking at his heels. Meanwhile Ganny, to whom this is all foolishness, has taken herself to the porch.

Out on the sidewalks the crowds are gathering, neighbors and tourists and old Bristolians back in town for the Glorious Fourth, and some of them are breaking away from the pack to open the garden gate. They're friends and acquaintances come to stand beneath the porch and chat with Ganny. None will call her Margaret. She is Mrs. Lonergan to everyone, just as her friends are Miss and Mrs. to her. That's how they go through life, fenced from one another by mutual formality, and although they're walking in the same direction, their shoulders never touch.

Gampa, off the balcony now and pulling out his pipe on the front steps, is Tom to everybody. But he, too, keeps his distance, his only true cronies being Old Man Connery, Old Man Connors (I will never know their first names) and Ralph Kinder, the florist, for whom he enjoys doing odd jobs. Gampa would like to have some eggnog, but he knows better. Once some Thames Street—that's the street that runs along the waterfront—tosspots lured him into the Hurricane Bar, and he had to be escorted home. Diana and I watched from the window while they hauled him stumbling up the front steps, and he went to bed in disgrace. Ganny walked around with thinned lips; Mother, always nervous of what people might think, was cold and dismissive: and Diana, who thought it was funny, called him "Hurricane" for weeks.

Drums are pounding in the distance, and cops on motorcycles are coming around the corner of Summer Street. Here they are: the Fourth of July Committee, swinging their canes and doffing their hats, the Colt Memorial High School

Band (one day Ruthie will be drum major) in their spanking green and white, Bristol's own bugle-and-drum corps, straight-backed, small-buttocked, bugles high and blatting.

Fife-and-drum corps in colonial outfits. Two men and a boy in tatters and bandages portraying the Spirit of '76. The *Quarante et Huit*, World War I veterans packed into a boxcar, plump and cheering. Shriners looking silly in their silks and fezzes. (One of the Barrington crowd is wearing his fez and three-fingers a conspiratorial salute.) Cesar B., Bristol's richest *brava*, his brass-colored skin tarnished in the cold northern light, prancing on his palomino. Over all, the flag with the anchor that says "Hope" and the flag with the severed snake that says "Don't tread on me."

A wail, many wails, and the fire engines are bringing up the rear, with the boys of Bristol hanging from them like monkeys do from trees. Now Di and I can brush the grass off our shorts and hazard the bathrooms which, on Mother's order, have been the exclusive property of the Barrington crowd, not one of whom, she says, can hold it. Above us balloons have tangled themselves in the trees or drifted upward to push against the sky until they're out of sight, and their temporary custodians are sobbing into the lawn.

The afternoon is as flat as if someone has put a lid on it. Papa and Mother are at the chief marshall's reception; Esther is off somewhere with one of the girls from the shop; Ganny is in her rocker, scouring the *Providence Journal*; and Gampa is on the Connerys' back steps talking to Old Man

Connery. There is nothing for Di and me to do but sit in the playroom, packing and unpacking the trunks of our Dy-Dee dolls, reading our Judy Morton books, and coloring our entries to the Dixie Dugan dress-design contest. Until Gampa decides, that is, that the air has cooled and the sun is low enough for us to go up to the Common and the carnival.

Summer's heat has settled on the Common and the yellow dust rises up to meet it, sifting through our sandals and our socks and lodging between our toes. Gampa buys us cotton candy, which sticks to our faces, and orange soda, which stains our mouths, and stands between our mounts on the merry-go-round. We are really too old for the merry-go-round, but he is not, and he is grinning as what he calls the dobby horses plunge up and down and the Common spins around us.

The games are shaded by a square of canvas tethered to four poles and we stand in the umber light with the rest of Bristol's gamblers, tossing pennies into numbered squares and rings around milk bottles. Next we try to fool the man who guesses weights by puffing our cheeks, and get our fortunes told by a battered automaton in a windowed box. A tall dark man is in my future. We peer into the trailers housing what all Bristol believes to be Gypsies, and we jump—Gampa, too—if any of their inhabitants glance in our direction. Certainly they look like Gypsies, these dark-haired, sallow people who run the carnival, and we shiver

MARY CANTWELL

in the face of the footloose. "They leave signs, y'know, when they travel on," Gampa says, "but only another Gypsy can read them."

The Ferris wheel is the centerpiece of the carnival, and we save it for last, settling into the gently swaying seats with a sigh. Our feet are sore and our eyes runny and we have breathed too long of dust and cotton candy and motor oil. Up here, though, up here on the top of the Ferris wheel, our faces are brushed by the salt-laced wind that is fingering the tops of the elms. With Gampa, whose arms enclose us, we survey our domain. Bristol lies before us, as neat and tidy as it would appear on an aerial map.

If we look to the left we can see the greasy-pole contest and the water fight between the fire battalions and, behind them, lowering over Wood Street, St. Mary's Church, its rectory, and the convent for the parochial school nuns. Down on the corner is the old town cemetery, its worn gravestones half-swallowed by tall, coarse grass. "How many people are dead in there?" Papa likes to sing out as we walk toward church on Sunday. "All of them!" we chorus.

We can see the bandstand in the center of the Common, and the men setting up the folding chairs for the concert to be given by the Portuguese Independent Band. Our Lady of Mount Carmel, the Italian church, is to the right, and beyond it we can see the spires of St. Elizabeth's, the Portuguese church.

The Walley School is straight ahead, windows closed, shades drawn, silent as a clam. A strip of grass separates it from the Baptist church, and a broader strip runs between the church and the old courthouse. At the corner the Byfield School stares at the Reynolds School across the street, each of them as shuttered and as secret as the Walley. If we could peer through the trees that fringe the Common—but no, the leaves are too thick in summer—we could see Bristol Harbor, and sailboats on their last tack.

The sun is setting, and the men of the Portuguese Independent Band have taken their seats in the bandstand. A drum roll, and "Lady of Spain" crashes through the still, hot air. Fireworks star the sky and Roman candles shoot up from the backyards on Wood Street.

It's time to walk home, past porches from which we can hear low voices and the squeak of gliders, and see cigarettes glowing in the dark. Soon we'll be on our own porch, spooning up coffee ice cream from Buffington's and listening to the boom of fireworks from over Poppasquash way.

With the sun gone, the air is damp as a used towel, and the scent of low tide is drifting up from the foot of Union Street. The cars have all gone back to Providence and Taunton and maybe even as far as Boston, and the cleaning trucks have already swept through town. Di and I are perched on the porch railing, and Ganny and Gampa are settled in their wicker chairs; and the coffee ice cream is puddling in Ganny's little glass bowls. "Isn't this a nice party?" Gampa says, happy because he wants no more at this moment than this wife, these grandchildren, and this house. "Please," Diana begs, "please, please do 'O, dem golden slippers.' "

MARY CANTWELL

Tall, thin Gampa hoists short, fat Ganny out of her chair and bang! goes the screen door as we trail inside. We take our seats and Gampa positions himself in front of the fireplace. Then, his feet sliding and scuffling through imaginary sand, he half-sings, half-whispers "O, dem golden slippers, O, dem golden slippers . . ." and sketches out a softshoe. Di and I applaud, Ganny's mouth curls at the corners. "Slapjack!" Diana commands, and we move into the dining room, to sit around the golden oak table, enclosed in the light from the amber-shaded chandelier, with a pack of tired cards. Screams, and flattened palms smacking the piles of cards and finally, after Ganny finishes rinsing the ice cream dishes, a foursome of whist.

A clatter at the front door. Mother and Papa are home after a lobster dinner with the Barrington crowd, and Esther is due any minute from God knows where. We look up, startled, and a little sad. Our club, the finest to which I will ever belong, is breaking up for the night.

Chapter Ten

On the day that John Fitzgerald Kennedy was assassinated I heard the news while standing in line at a bank in Grand Central Terminal. The day after Francis Gary Powers drifted into Soviet air space I was on a Greenwich Village street, pushing my firstborn child in her plaid baby carriage and praying. "Dear God," I pleaded, "she's only had six weeks."

On the day that Franklin Delano Roosevelt died I was frightened, because he had been my president for about as long as Papa had been my father, and, with God, together they made up my own Holy Trinity. But about that first big day in my lifetime, the day the Japanese bombed Pearl Harbor, I'm uncertain.

Sometimes I can see my parents at the radio and hear the announcer's excited stutter. But did I really? After all, I can see the Hindenberg hovering over the foot of Union Street too, while Diana, the Tingley boys, and I stare breathless at the sky. It hung there like a big black cigar. But maybe not. Maybe I had only seen a photograph. No matter. If I can claim to have seen the Hindenberg, then I can claim that on Pearl Harbor Day I was taking my usual Sunday afternoon walk. And in truth I was so faithful to ritual—the season's first horse chestnut in my pocket to ward off rheumatism, the same five prayers recited every night—I probably was.

In my story, then, I'm heading south, the harbor at my right and a horse chestnut in my coat pocket. As soon as I get to where Wood Street, still wild and overgrown at its southern end, runs into Hope Street and both become Ferry Road I will turn and start back for *The Shadow* and supper in the kitchen. Now, however, I'm passing Union Street, where some men in a skiff are taking up eels with what look like long forks. I'm passing the Lee School, which is banked in Sunday silence, and Burton Street, where the cement sidewalk turns into a narrow gravel path; and the Herreshoff boatyards, where two America's Cup Defenders, stripped of their masts and swaddled in tarps, present their sterns to the passerby.

Just beyond the Lobster Pot, the restaurant Mother and Papa go to with the Barrington crowd on Friday nights, I pause to lean on a cement-surfaced stone wall, another of the WPA's gifts to Bristol, and look at the harbor. I am always looking at the harbor and someday I want to be buried beside it, at the foot of Walley Street, in the brilliant green grass that precedes the drop to a small shingle. There

AMERICAN GIRL

I'll be toe to toe with Indian bones, and gazing out at Poppasquash.

The harbor is naked today of all but the Prudence Island ferry, and the sun is an orange ball falling slowly behind Hog Island. Below me the water is washing over barnacled rocks and speckled pebbles and rubbery strands of seaweed. Several seagulls are circling over the ruins of a breakwater and look! There's a rat slipping into a crack in the wall.

I walk on, and spongy grass takes over for gravel. The harbor disappears as the coastline moves westward, the trees thicken and the air goes from salt to something damp, moldy and ineffably sad. Wet leaves are sticking to the soles of my shoes now, so I cross the street to higher, drier ground, face north, and slowly amble home. Did I get to hear *The Shadow*, or was the radio tuned to the news? I know only that the streets of Bristol weren't that empty again for a long, long time. And that I was about to commence my education in sex and reproduction.

It was the sailors. They were stationed in Newport, twelve miles away, and looking for something to do. "Here's a nickel, honey," they'd sing out to kids, myself among them, as they hopped off the Shoreline bus, bold and bandy-legged and bent on the Belvedere. "Call me up in five years."

Bristol basked in the grandeur of being a possible target for any bombers and a landing point for any submarines that might manage to slither across the Atlantic. We were prepared. Each night we drew the curtains and pulled the cords on the venetian blinds and Gampa stepped forth on patrol, a tin hat on his head, a flashlight in his hand, a whistle clenched between his false teeth. Let just one streak of light escape a blind and Gampa would shriek the careless householder into shame.

Uncle John, the youngest of Ganny and Gampa's children, was with the Navy in the South Pacific, a great relief to his parents because this was the first time in years they'd been sure of his whereabouts. There was little of Uncle John at 232 Hope Street, only a few pictures of a sharp dresser with a pipe in his mouth, some old phonograph records— Kid Ory and His Creole Jazz, Red Nichols and His Five Copper Pennies—and a big polished shell that said "Pitcairn Islands." Whenever I asked Mother and Esther about my dashing young uncle, known to one and all as "Red" because of his russet hair, their faces snapped shut like purses.

Diana and I had dogtags in case of evacuation, but Ganny figured we could sit out anything. To her, war was the equivalent of the lines coming down, and she was ready for it. Let a bomb strike the Narragansett Electric Light Company, and she'd bring out the kerosene lamps, put the milk and butter in the ice box in the back entry and fire up the coal stove. Let the water mains collapse and it would be necessary only to pry up the slab that had sealed Miss Munro's well for these past fifty years and lo! there was water enough to flush our toilets into the next century.

When I think of us as we were then, every image that

AMERICAN GIRL

surfaces seems straight out of *Life* and *The Saturday Evening Post*. We are clichés, all of us.

There's me marching to the front of the classroom every week to deposit a dollar in my Defense Bond account. Papa coming home from trips to New York for U.S. Rubber with tales of standing room only so he had to sit on his suitcase all the way to Grand Central, and no rooms at the Biltmore so he had to stay in some fleabag on the other side of town. Ganny puzzling out the ration books through her magnifying glass. Diana, who had memorized a book on airplane identification, crouched in the bushes that hid the red-brick foundation of 232 Hope Street and scanning the skies for the Luftwaffe. Gampa leaving home in helmet and raincoat for his evening patrol. Mother making a face as she crushed the orangy-yellow pellet into the lardy oleo to make it look like butter.

One afternoon she saw a little boy walk past the house with a brick of real butter in his hand. He'd taken off the paper wrapper and was licking it like an ice cream cone. If I could not still hear her voice telling the story—"Oh, I tell you, he made me laugh," she says—I would think him a figment of Norman Rockwell's imagination. Such homely images, however, don't account for the change in the weather, my sense that we were always on the verge of an electrical storm. It was as if those sailors swarming through town charged the air.

Whenever I walked up street now, my ears were pricked for the whispered invitation—"How's about you and me stepping around the corner for a beer?" If it had come, I'd have turned it down. I'd have drawn back affronted. I would have fixed that sailor with a cold stare, I would, and smiled inside my skin. But I was safe, and I knew it. I was young, too young to attract, too young to be guilty of being sexy.

I saw them going down to Newport for dinner at the Officers' Club, the nice Bristol girls with the pageboys and the Peck & Peck sweaters and the flat cigarette cases. An officer's uniform constituted a social bona fide, so the cocktail parties down the Ferry were thronged with young men in spotless white uniforms and gold-braided caps, and there was always what my mother called "a good-looking crowd" at the bar of the Lobster Pot. Even Esther, in her thirties now and feigning horror when Diana and I stuck her with the Old Maid card, stained her bare legs brown and painted her mouth with Germaine Monteil's Beauty Red and shared manhattans and lobster Newburgs with a balding lieutenant named Stoner.

But the sailors! Who knew who they were, in their funny little bell-bottoms with their funny little fronts that let down like trapdoors to reveal the reason they were hopping from buses and packing the Thames Street bars? Sailors had to make do with Bugeyes and Margie.

Bugeyes, whose legs bowed and whose eyes bulged, was new to Bristol. But we knew Margie. Everybody knew Margie. Margie was terrifying.

Margie's mother, Gladys, was a cleaning lady. Ganny

said she'd been with the circus, but Ganny had a way of providing people with backdrops. Because her father came from Canada, for instance, she liked to claim he was an Eskimo. That Gladys was small and wiry and hennaed her hair and buttered her mouth with magenta lipstick was cause enough for Ganny to put her in spangles. But then again, maybe she was with the circus. Nobody knew where she came from, only that her husband slid, drunk probably, in front of a car and that Margie was their only child.

The pear trees in our backyard were prodigious bearers, and in August, when they sagged with fruit, passing children asked to pick it. When she was small, Margie was among them. Agile as a monkey, she flew from branch to branch, plucking the pears and tossing them to the grass beneath. Seeing her up there against the sky one could indeed believe her mother had swung on a trapeze and spanned the ceiling of the big tent. On the ground, though, she was a foul-mouthed fireplug of a girl with hair the color of dingy brass. Margie and Gladys looked like the people who worked the carnival booths—sallow, stringy, and dusty—and although they lived in a house on Constitution Street they seemed more suited to a trailer.

Margie had a temper. She pounded on Bristol as if it were a cage, and no one was safe from that terrible anger. One afternoon after school let out she growled Ruthie and me, who had stayed up on the Common to shoot marbles, up the steps of the bandstand and into a corner. "Don't you

ever look at me again, you little bitches," she screamed.
When she walked away her heels struck sparks off the pavement and her anger stained the air.

So of course Margie grew up to prance down Hope
Street with a sailor on her arm, trapped-up and high-
stepping as a circus pony. "Don't you dare look at me," her
fierce eyes said, and nobody did. Blindness overtook Bristol
whenever Margie strutted through downtown: to glance was
to risk a scolding from that boiling tongue.

What she did, she did for seats at the Pastime or beers
at the Belvedere or to rattle the bars of the cage, and she
did it constantly, brazenly, ferociously. "Guess what I saw
this afternoon?" Diana whispered from her bed one night.
She had seen Margie dive off the Coast Guard dock and
swim the twenty or so yards to where a boat and some sailors
were waiting, cheering, to haul her aboard.

We knew what Margie did. We knew what our parents
did too, although we refused to believe it. Once, poking
about in Papa's top drawer, I found a package of something
called Trojans, recognized them for the rubbers I had heard
some boys talking about, and felt a strange, slow tearing
down my chest. Not my father. No!

Another time, while I was on one of my secret, silent
prowls of the house, prowls in which I opened purses and
thumbed through my mother's lingerie and plundered the
desk for traces of the life my parents lived without my knowing it, I climbed upon a chair and ran my criminal fingers
along a shelf in their bedroom closet. Van de Velde's *Ideal*

Marriage was up there, hidden behind a set of hatboxes. Only a few minutes elapsed before I heard Mother coming up from downstairs, but they were long enough for me to read about the Mound—or was it the Mount?—of Venus and how the pubic hair of women in obscure parts of the world sometimes grew to enormous length. When, a few months later, tiny circles of brown hair began appearing on my pubis, I lay in bed at night, my hand on the forbidden place, and stubbornly, painfully pulled them out.

One morning I found my underpants stiff with rusty, iron-smelling blood, and cried that I had lost my innocence. Mother and Esther rigged me a sanitary belt out of a torn-up old sheet and two safety pins, and said it meant I was turning into a big girl. Esther said she'd run up to the five-and-ten and get me a box of Modess. "I always ask for a box of candy," she said, "and the salesgirl knows what I mean." Mother said "whatchamaycallit" lasted for four or five days.

For a long time I sat on the toilet, not trusting that torn-up sheet, and watched the water in the bowl turn red. I wasn't safe anymore. I was the same as Margie now. Both of us wore pads between our thighs, both of us sported the same curly patch. We were similarly disgusting.

Eventually the worst thing that could happen to anybody happened to Margie. I heard about it the way I heard about everything, by lurking unobserved next to the sliding doors that separated Ganny's two parlors. "Guess who's expecting?" Esther said to her when she came home from the shop one autumn night. "And guess what Gladys is telling everybody? She says it's just that Margie drank some canned grapefruit juice that had gone bad, and that it made her swell up."

A few days later Ganny sent me to Buffington's for corn plasters. Just to the left of the entrance was the toiletries display, chaste rows of Elizabeth Arden creams and face powders, my mother's favorites and as evocative of her as Germaine Monteil's thick satiny lipsticks were of Esther. My mother even looked like the woman in the ads, the woman with the marble skin and the mummy wrappings around her head. The door opened and let in a gust of Juicy Fruit gum, laundry soap, and Bourjoie's Evening in Paris, familiar to me because it was sold, in tasseled blue vials, at the five-and-ten. Margie. I could see her reflection in the glass.

She walked to the prescription counter in the rear of the store and stood with her back to me. If I turned my head just a little bit I could see the bulge, the telltale swell of sin. No, too dangerous. Breathless, I stared at that evocation of order and austerity that was Elizabeth Arden cosmetics until a slam of the door announced that chaos had left the store.

Margie and Gladys were never seen in Buffington's, or anywhere else in Bristol, again. Esther heard they'd left town on the early bus, and I pictured them in the wet gray dawn, Margie's bulge buttoned into that big coat and their luggage bumping against their legs. I pictured them, too, on bleak city streets and in theatrical boardinghouses and dragging themselves, down at the heels, through dreary rail-road stations: the stuff of countless Saturday afternoons at the Pastime Theater.

Margie was gone and Bugeyes dissolved back into wherever it was she came from, but the sailors were still there, still bounding off the bus and keeping an eye open for a girl who might split a beer and take them off the streets they were so hopelessly strolling. One late afternoon one of them approached Diana.

Tall for her age, she was up on the Common, poking along on her long, bird legs, when he asked her how she'd like a tumble. She came home crying. What was there about her that made him think she'd do something like that? "It's your own fault," I said. "You never look like you know where you're going. You should walk faster, and quit drifting about the way you do."

"I'll try," she sobbed, and thus I shifted the blame for an insult from a randy sailor to a child's blameless but unmistakably female back.

Chapter Eleven

It is still there, the Pastime Theater, only now it's called the Bristol Cinema and is divided into two narrow screening rooms. Tickets are very cheap and the shows change twice a week. Even so the Bristol Cinema is always up for sale, always rumored to be closing. Nobody, except for the very old and a few little kids, goes to the movies anymore. There was a time, though, when Bristolians attended the Pastime as regularly as they attended church. It was, in fact, the only place in town where Protestants and Catholics didn't feel the one was getting an edge on the other.

My parents said it was really Joanie's aunt who ran the Pastime, that the man who owned it couldn't have managed without her. She sold the tickets and, trotting across the tiny lobby, sold the candy, and on Saturday afternoons walked the aisles after the curtain went up, flashing a light on whoever was tossing spitballs or whistling through his fingers or squabbling with the kids in the next row. I was a regular at the Saturday matinee, bouncing on the cracked leather seats, gumming up my teeth with jujubes and dodging the flashlight, drunk on the darkness and the big screen and the pervasive salt/grease smell of Spanish peanuts. I loved the serial, the cartoon, the newsreel, the Fitzgerald travelogue, the Pete Smith specialty, the feature, and whatever served as dessert—the Three Stooges usually, but once a short of black men sitting in a row, knees pressed together, singing "Dem bones, dem bones, dem dry bones," that had me chanting "The thigh bone connecka to the knee bones and the knee bones connecka to the . . ." for weeks thereafter.

When the fast-talking daughter of the fat lady who lived on Byfield Street eloped with the sailor she'd picked up in Providence, her mother proclaimed that all was forgiven by appearing with them at the Friday night movies. When a couple started going together they announced it by their presence at the Friday night movies. When people recovered from illness or came out of mourning, the first place they went was the Friday night movies.

In summertime the Ferry crowd showed up, Shetland sweaters looped over their spanking white shirts, Sperry Topsiders lending a bounce to their walk. The big cheeses from Colt Memorial High—football players and cheerleaders and honor-roll students whose names were always in *The Bristol Phoenix*—jammed the aisles, and the kids who lived up the Neck arrived in a body. If the feature starred

Bette Davis the grownups from the country of the blue-eyed came, too, and so, finally, did Di and I, graduated at last from the Saturday matinee but escorted by Gampa.

To Gampa, Diana and I were as dear as his cocker spaniel, Judy, and he looked at the three of us with the same loving eyes. Many were the nights we found him sitting in his morris chair sucking on his pipe while Judy gnawed blissfully at the hand he'd let dangle over the side. "You know how to tell when Gampa's talking to Ganny and when he's talking to Judy," we teased. "Judy's the one he calls 'darling.' "

When Joanie's aunt handed him the tickets, Gampa said "Thank you kindly" and ushered us to a row midway down the aisle. We sat on either side of him, and all three of us were smiling—he because he was going to see the picture show and Di and I because we were excited by the hustle and the bustle and the smack of the wadded-up candy wrapper in the back of the neck that announced that somewhere in this theater was somebody who had a crush on one of us. (One night I looked down our row past Gampa and saw a boy with eyes as blue as bachelor buttons. He returned my look, laughing, and I knew for the first time— as did he, I learned a few years later—what it is to feel your heart dissolve.) Then the lights dimmed, the red velvet curtain went up, Movietone News sounded its salute and we were lifted out of our seats and deposited, gently, in heaven. Betty Grable flashed her flawless knees; Dan Dailey grinned his loopy grin. "That Dan Dailey," Gampa whispered. "He's a hummer!"

By the time the Pastime let out it was nearly eleven and the streets were deserted. Most of the houses were dark and sleeping, and the few cars that sped along Hope Street were, we figured, rushing the sick to the hospital in Providence or rushing for the last train out of Rhode Island. Why else would anyone be driving so long after sundown? Buffington's, however, was open and crowded.

The high school kids were lined up at the marble counter calling for lemon Cokes and Dusty Roads, and the air was thick with the whir of mixers, the squawk of the soda pull, and the thuds of the covers on the ice cream cases. Invariably, Gampa paused out front and asked if we wanted cones. We blushed at the picture he'd make in there—an old man in a three-piece suit among the gods—and worried lest somebody looked out the door and saw us, two young girls and their grandfather, peering in at Olympus. Someday, I knew, I'd be in there too, sipping a Coke and tossing back my pageboy. But not now, not yet. Comfortable in my chrysalis, I pulled at Gampa's hand and we walked on, toward the light that Ganny had left burning over the front door and the sleep that would bring me one day closer to my blooming.

My blooming, my blooming. In just a few more years I would be part of the Friday night crowd at Buffington's

Drugstore and of the great mass that moved slowly down High Street after the football games at Guiteras Field. My breasts would bud and my hair turn under at the ends, and the faint scattering of pimples across my forehead would have succumbed forever to Acnomel. All that was to come, and it *would* come some day, some day when I was older: when I, like Ruthie, had personality; when I, like my mother before me, entered Colt Memorial High School. For now, though, there was hearing the factory whistle blow at noon and the town clock peal the hours and knowing how to translate the fire alarm's telltale honks. There was Alger's Newsstand and the penny-candy store next to the firehouse and the Rogers Free Library, where I studied the shelves for Gene Stratton Porter and Rafael Sabatini and sat at its golden oak tables turning the pages of *Life*. But above all there was my father. When I walked uptown with him of a Saturday morning, through the buzz and the busyness and the slams of car doors and shouts of "Ay paysan!" from workmen he knew at the shop, I was as shaken by joy as if it held me in its teeth.

He was born in North Brookfield, Massachusetts, but grew up in Fall River, a city so dingy its very name was a pejorative. "When we were kids," my mother would say, "and somebody said something dirty we'd say 'Oh, that's Fall River!' " But Papa could turn dross into gold, the merely dreary into Hell. When he sat on the toybox at night, talking Diana and me to sleep, we clamored for Fall River as we would have for ghost stories.

AMERICAN GIRL

"In the mills, the floors were so slippery with cottonseed oil that all the boys worked barefoot. The men were mostly English, with bad teeth, and all of them had redheaded wives. I swear! I can see them now, those redheads, coming down the hills with their husbands' tin lunch pails when the noon whistle blew."

Yes, Fall River has hundreds of redheaded women who descended its hills like brushfires, not to mention a remarkable boulder that an Ice-Age glacier deposited there on its trek down the Atlantic seaboard. But, then, everything in Fall River is remarkable. A woman whom Papa knew as a child had a terrible disease that turned her to stone; that's the kind of place Fall River is. His father's cousin, Dr. Kelly's wife, lived next door to the Borden family and was the last person to see Andrew Jackson Borden alive. A crime like that—well, that's Fall River for you. Rich textile tycoons lived washed in cool breezes atop Fall River's seven hills, while the poor sweltered in the heat below and the air hummed day and night with the sound of spinning. When you crossed the bridge from Somerset and entered the city, a cloud descended and wrapped you in its folds. Fall River! The heart sinks.

"Tell us about the policeman who used to chase you," we'd ask, wriggling deeper into our pillows.

"Martin Quigley. He was tough. You see, I was bad, *really* bad. After school I'd hang around under the street lamp with a bunch from the neighborhood. We'd stay out way past our bedtime, and run and hide when our mothers called us in. Then Martin Quigley would come and chase us home."

Delighted that our father had been bad, we'd squirm. (I can still feel that squirm, that small joyous spasm, because I still squirm when I'm happy, when someone—a writer, say, or Fred Astaire—does something and does it dead-on.) "Did your mother think you'd been bad?"

"Ahhhh," and his voice would grow suddenly, atavistically Irish. "I wish you'd known her. She was six feet tall and had snapping black eyes. They were all tall, both sides. My father's mother, also six feet tall, ran around Glasgow on Orangeman's Day tearing down the orange flags. She was a Catholic, and she didn't like those damn Presbyterians."

More joy than we could handle. We were the descendants of heroes. We slept as if couched on zephyrs.

"Of course, I'm a carpetbagger in Bristol," Papa told me more than once, "not like your mother's family. And I'll always be a carpetbagger. Like that Joe who applied for the janitor's job at the Reynolds. Did I ever tell you what happened to Joe?

"His application came up before the School Committee and it looked to me as if he was as suitable as anybody else. Hell, all he had to do was push a broom. But somebody said, 'No, I think we ought to give the job to a native.'

"So I said, 'I thought Joe was a native.' Not by their standards! 'Leo,' they said, 'Joe didn't come to Bristol until he was three months old.'

AMERICAN GIRL

"Can you beat it, Mary Lee?" he said, his outflung arm taking in St. Michael's Church and the clapboard houses and the old soaks hanging around the entrance to the Belvedere Hotel as we strolled up Hope Street. "Can you beat this town for craziness?"

Taking a walk with Papa was like looking out the bay window with Ganny. Because of them I, too, saw my fellow Bristolians as participants in an enormous parade that marched daily, and for my benefit.

"There is little more beautiful in this world, Mary Lee, than the sun sinking into Bristol Harbor. You and your sister are very fortunate to live in a place like this. Why, people go on vacation to places like this." Papa waves his arm again.

In places like this the main street is one big living room. Here they come, for instance, the old maids of Bristol, all of them converging on the Rogers Free Library where they will exchange a Frances Parkinson Keyes for a Mazo de la Roche, or a Mazo de la Roche for a Frances Parkinson Keyes. Louise DeWolf, a high school classmate of my mother's, is here, shod as usual in sneakers that call attention to the fact that her legs appear to have been put on upside down. So is Miss Alice Morgan, who has sojourned in Istanbul, wrapped in a long flowing cape; and Miss Bourn, who had been engaged to a German nobleman until her father lost his little rubber works, with her mesh evening purse over her arm; and our neighbor, Miss Belle Bosworth, her hair in a pouf, her dress to her ankles, her late father's watch on a chain around her neck, and her long ivory hand twirling a parasol. One block to the south, Miss Evvie Bache, descendant of Benjamin Franklin and terrible housekeeper, is picking her way through the stacks of old newspapers and mounds of cat vomit that litter her eighteenth-century house. (I know, because I was sent there once to borrow costumes—I was Martha Washington in a Bache ancestor's ancient sprigged dimity—for the fifth-grade history pageant and threw up upon leaving.) "Mary Lee," Papa says, "I hope to God you marry when you grow up."

Now we are in the library, and Papa is asking for the best-seller the librarians have hidden under the counter for him. They are two of Joanie's aunts: Swedish, blond, and spinsters all. A third aunt is the wonder that runs the Pastime Theater and a fourth aunt keeps a firm hand on the second grade up at the Walley School. That makes the area bounded by State, Bradford, Hope, and High Streets, Papa says, the Kingdom of the Osterbergs.

One of the Miss Osterbergs slips him the new A. J. Cronin. "They say it's very good," she whispers. Conversations at the library never rise above funeral-home level: The Osterberg sisters are fast with a "shhhh" and an upraised index finger. They are also so neat and clean—"Swedes always look like that," my mother claims—I think they polish themselves with a chamois before they leave the house in the morning.

"They" who pronounce on books are Ralph Kinder, the superintendant of schools, and the minister of St. Michael's Church who, along with Papa, are the library's best readers.

AMERICAN GIRL

Some of Papa's glory rubs off on his children. The Osterbergs deem certain books unsuitable for certain age groups, but they allow me a little leeway. For instance I am permitted Kathleen Winsor and Thomas B. Costain, since the sisters figure I'm reading them for the history. Anybody else my age would be looking for the dirty parts.

Miss Osterberg stamps Papa's card, and motions him closer. "I'm getting in the new O'Hara next week." Papa beams. "Mary Lee, I'm a lucky guy."

Papa's kingdom is on Wood Street. It's the U. S. Rubber Company, where he is production manager. He cannot stay away from the shop, even on Saturdays when only the factory workers are on hand. To go there we stroll east on Bradford Street, past Colt Memorial High School and the house he and Mother lived in when they were first married.

"It was on those steps that I was sitting on the night you were born and your mother and your great-aunt Annie were turning the town upside down looking for me. Wouldn't you think one of them would have had the sense to stick her head out the window?" He laughs fondly and I laugh with him, smug in the knowledge that I am a true Cantwell, and that the family into which he married and to which I am related is—however handsome—feckless, absent-minded, and no real part of us. A Cantwell would have had the sense to look out the window.

The entrance to the U.S. Rubber Company is spanned by a red-brick arch, and a watchman sits in at little tower at its right. Papa waves a grand, seigneurial wave and steers me past a time clock and row after row of little yellow cards and up a broad staircase to a big, empty room. While he's in his office checking out the production sheets, I stay in the clerks' bull pen, delirious among the pads and pencils and typewriters and comptometers and ditto machines, the last of which I can work because he showed me how. I love the very smell of them, the effluvium—sharp and very clean—that rises from paper and ink and metal type. In fifth grade I printed a homeroom newspaper on one of the ditto machines, but it only lasted one issue. "If we're going to have a newspaper," the teacher said, "we've got to do it properly and elect an editor in chief." I wasn't elected. I wasn't even nominated, and the person who was never produced a follow-up. "Never mind," Papa said when I cried so hard I was sick. "Someday you'll live in a place where there are lots of people like you."

Papa is finished with the production sheets. "C'mon, Lulubelle," he calls. "Let's go see what the factory's doing."

The factory is doing war work, so the men are battening on overtime. The spinners are whirring and the extruders are squeezing out long, fat rubber worms and we are above it all, up on the catwalks looking down on Papa's kingdom. "Ay Leo! Ay coompah!" somebody yells up to him. Papa waves, and inhales the stink of rubber as joyously as another man would sniff a rose.

Better get home. He's got a golf game this afternoon, and then he and Mother are going to a dinner dance at the Rhode Island Country Club with the Barrington crowd.

They're stopping at our house first, though, for a few of Papa's famous old-fashioneds. I, who am a nuisance, will hang around to watch him—tall and plump in a dark Brooks Brothers suit ("Put me in tweed," he says, "and I look like a racetrack tout"), a gold watch chain swagging his stomach. His hazel eyes, which are roofed with thick, black brows, will be fixed on the sugar cubes he is crushing, and when it comes time to shake in the Angostura he'll be as careful as a chemist. "*Nosdorovya!*" he'll say when he extends the glasses. "Bottoms up!"

We cross the Common, hand in hand. I am really too old to hold a parent's hand, but I cannot bear to give his up. When I was a baby, he—natty in a navy-blue jacket and ice-cream pants—flourished me for Miss Emilie Connery's camera, and even now I feel that I am still riding his shoulder. "Hurry up there, Lulubelle." I double my footsteps to match his stride. "They'll be wondering if we ran away."

Chapter Twelve

When the tide came in at Union Street it gobbled up the Popsicle sticks and greasy paper bags and soda bottles the afternoon crowd had left behind and carted them out to Narragansett Bay. I was like that tide, gobbling up Bristol street by street. Summer was when I was hungriest, during the long light days when the world asked nothing more of me than that I be home in time for dinner.

Summer, everybody said, was when Bristol couldn't be beat. On Back Road the air was stiff and sullen, and uptown the sun had baked the sidewalks. But once you crossed Court Street you were strolling through green tunnels. By the time you reached Constitution a salt breeze had sprung up, and by the time you neared Union you could hear the screams of swimmers. Sailboats bucked and winged around the harbor, and if the yacht club was holding a regatta, the deep blue water was thick with Herreshoff bull's-eyes and snipes and catamarans, bowing and curvetting and tugged by urgent spinnakers.

AMERICAN GIRL

Sometimes it was enough to spend the morning at Union Street, and the afternoon sprawled on the porch glider with a book balanced on my chest. More often, though, I was wandering the streets, peering into windows and trying to see into backyards. When anyone moved in or out of a house I was among the group on the sidewalk watching the furniture go by. It was as if Bristol were a book I couldn't put down.

If Bristol's population was small, the town itself was big. There was much of it I hadn't seen, still haven't seen for that matter. So when I heard about a farm up on the Back Road that hired kids to pick raspberries during the season, I begged to go. The Back Road, miles from our house and the harbor and everything I knew, would be a new chapter.

On a map the stretch of two-lane highway that connected Warren to the Mount Hope Bridge bore King Philip's Indian name, Metacom. But only a stranger would have called it Metacom Avenue. To everyone else it was the Back Road.

At its Warren end the Back Road was a squeeze of shabby houses, gas stations, and greenhouses. But as the road ran south toward Newport it opened into fields. Beyond the fields, a mile or so from the road, ran an inlet known as the Narrows and a pebbly beach lined with modest vacation cottages. Their owners showed up at St. Mary's Church on summer Sundays along with the cooks and maids from the big houses down the Ferry, most of whose employers were bowing their heads a few blocks away at St. Michael's.

The Old Soldiers' Home was on the Back Road, as was the estate of a Providence beer baron and the shipshape white clapboard of a retired rear admiral. But the only part of that long, lonely blacktop that I can claim to know is an acre or so of raspberry bushes.

A picture postcard, one of a group of old cards I found at Alger's Newsstand and saved, shows a whale's jawbone framing the entrance to the farm. I never saw it, what with always having to keep my eyes on the raspberries I was trying to yank from their canes, but it signified social status more surely than money ever could. The farm's owner, a homely red-haired woman descended from one of Bristol's first settlers, had whalers among her ancestors. In southern New England that beat out a Rockefeller any day.

She was married to the Portuguese field hand she'd put through college, and their four daughters took after him. They were handsome, like he was, and rumored to be foolish about men. When they rode their horses in the Fourth of July parade they topped their chignoned heads with flat-brimmed sombreros, and their mounts jingled silver trappings. If Bristol had had a café society they'd have been in it.

The pickers, none of them besides myself from the country of the blue-eyed, met near St. Mary's soon after daybreak, crawled into the back of a pick-up truck and were deposited ten minutes later at a stone wall by which a dark-haired woman in halter and shorts was waiting. The couple's second daughter, she slapped a riding crop against her bare legs and stalked the rows with the zeal with which her ancestors, who were also in the slave trade, had stalked their ships.

For each basket filled we were to be paid five cents, she said, and each of us could take one home. But if somebody driving by, somebody, she implied, from out of town, were to offer to buy our berries, we had to say no. Not only would we be depriving our families of their supper treat, but we would be depriving her family of business that they would have had but for their generosity in allowing us to take a pint of berries. We nodded solemnly, we bent our backs, the sun slapped us on the shoulders.

While his daughter prowled the rows, her father, magnificent in a mustache, white suit, and Panama hat, stood smiling broadly, a gold tooth glinting in the sun, and waited for us to bring him our baskets to be counted. Sometimes, a fellow picker whispered, he gave the prettiest girls a feel. It was an honor. "He's my uncle," the Portuguese kids said, or "He's my father's cousin . . . my mother's brother-in-law's relation." He was a big man among the Portuguese, famous for his good looks and his dashing daughters and his flourishing farm. I halfway hoped he'd give me a feel, but I never even got a glance. Maybe I'm not pretty enough, I told myself, but I knew I was. More likely he trailed his long elegant fingers, if he trailed them at all, only over those who shared his blood.

It was another world up there on the Back Road, so far from the harbor and the breeze and the persistent scent of salt. The air shuddered in the heat, and working so close to the ground I could smell nothing but dirt and berries. The other kids scrambled through the rows, serious about their picking, and soon I was serious too. Here, as everywhere, I wanted to be part of the gang, even of a gang whose names I seldom caught and with whom, given the rigid tracking of Bristol's public schools, I would never share a classroom. We seldom spoke, only tugged at those resistant raspberries and exchanged sheepish smiles when we caught sight of one another through the bushes.

Walking the three miles home through the drowsy afternoon, sunburned and scratched and sweaty, I was as happy as I had ever been. This suited me, this silent companionship and the wallowing in the dust before a dip in the harbor, a dip that would wash away the dirt and iodize the scraches and leave me with the face all Bristol children sported in summer: red-eyed, with a nose that dripped salt water. That fresh air was all that separated the Portuguese kids who were so happy to be working for a kinsman in a spotless white suit from the children who ran barefoot over the oil-slicked floors of the Fall River mills never entered my mind.

Ferry Road was only a stroll from 232 Hope Street, but in a way it was as inaccessible as the Back Road. More so, really. Its residents were barely glimpsed figures on Raleigh bicycles with hand brakes and, at cruising speed, a purr like a cat's; or passengers in wooden-sided beach wagons with the names of their houses discreetly stenciled on the driver's door; or among the guests at weddings at St. Michael's. Ruthie and I loved weddings, especially those at St. Michael's, with its solemnly tolling bell and tall trees and the crumbling old gravestones in its churchyard, and were sorry that we couldn't be married there. Not only did St. Mary's not have a clock, but you had to climb a mile of steps to get to the front door, and when you came out all you saw was that grubby Common and all you smelled was the rubber factory. But the bridal couples at St. Michael's emerged to a sidewalk dappled with shade and air that was scented with salt, and cars slowed and seemed to tip their hats as they passed the limousines lined up out front.

In winter the summer people lived in Providence and showed up regularly in the Sunday society section of *The Providence Journal*, which I had taken to reading because of the bridal pictures. Down at the Ferry they stuck pretty close to home, playing tennis and sunning themselves at the foot of Monkeywrench Lane, and the most conspicuous evidence of their presence were the cooks and maids in the back rows of St. Mary's at eleven o'clock mass. In truth, there was another sign, but it was heard not seen: the moans of Bristol's grocers. The rich never paid their bills until after Labor Day.

Actually they didn't do anything, at least nothing that I could see. When my friend Jeanne, who had a baby-sitting job down the Ferry, got the grippe, I bicycled down Monkeywrench Lane every morning for a week, to a big house with grounds that spilled into Narragansett Bay. While I sat by the water with her babies, their mother drifted about the lawn and in and out of the house. Somebody was cleaning, somebody else was cooking, I was minding the children, and she was as vagrant as floss from a milkweed pod.

In the town proper every person was a filament in an enormous web. When one thread shook, the entire web shuddered. Our next-door neighbor Belle Bosworth walked uptown to meet Jessie Molasky, the junior high school librarian, to exchange her copy of the previous Sunday's *New York Times Book Review* with the latter's copy of the *Herald-Tribune Book Review*. Ganny phoned her bookie. The Misses Osterberg, commanding the Rogers Free Library, forbade Ruthie *Forever Amber*. Even at midnight, when all sober Bristolians were in bed, the web shivered. But here there was no web, only figures moving across a landscape that, however much they paid for it and however many years they made their annual visit, they couldn't possibly possess.

To me dailiness was nine-tenths of possession, and how could anyone own something she knew only in the summer? How could anyone know Bristol if she didn't know that in autumn half its backyards flaunted winter cherries? Or that the Congregationalists put on the best Christmas fairs? Or that in spring the linden trees in front of the high school had a scent so sweet and haunting it was enough to make you cry? I didn't envy the summer people, although I coveted their bikes and wished my parents had a beach wagon like those they nosed through town. But it was I, not they, who

was a Bristolian—at least a Bristolian as they understood
the term. If I had ever heard myself described as a "local,"
I would have assumed it was a compliment.

There was only one place in Bristol proper besides St.
Michael's and, sometimes, the Pastime Theater, where the
summer people could be found. That was the Bristol Yacht
Club, a small and incongruous monument to International
Style at the foot of Constitution Street.

The old yacht club, a shingled nondescript, was lifted
off its perch by the Hurricane of '38 and shoveled into Bristol
Harbor. The old flagpole survived, or did until the night the
designer of the new yacht club, a middle-aged Bristolian
with flat feet and a famous name, had one too many and
chopped it down. Another night when he'd had another one
too many, he called the exchange and told the operator who
number-pleased him that he was going to bed but that she
could continue to put his calls through. His dog, a dachs-
hund whose low-bellied shuffle duplicated his, would
answer.

The new yacht club smelled of teak, leather, and salt,
which in coastal New England is the smell of money. Its
members were teak-colored, leather-skinned, and salt-
streaked, which in coastal New England is the look of
money. For the most part they—men with high-bridged
noses and long teeth and women whose freckled hands
flashed big old-fashioned diamonds—were around only for
the Saturday races. But during the week the yacht club
belonged to their children, and to a few of the children from

the country of the blue-eyed. Me, for instance, who was as eager to become a junior member of the Bristol Yacht Club as I had been to join the Girl Scouts.

We looked the same, we dressed the same, but we were not the same. I realized that the afternoon I was commandeered to pass the sandwiches at a yacht club tea. Not knowing I'd been positioned on the wrong side of the tea table, I was happy circulating my trays of egg-salad triangles and watching the S. sisters, cousins of the club's architect and famous tightwads, sliding theirs into their handbags. But after I boasted to Papa about how well I'd handled the trays he said, "Did———pass sandwiches?," naming the daughter of a pillar of St. Michael's. "Did ———?," naming another. When I answered no to both questions he said, "Then don't you ever do it again." He was furious, and I? I was as icy-spined as I was the day I found out I'd never be queen of England.

Once I'd propped my Schwinn in the gravel parking lot and entered that teak-smelling room, past the bulletin board with the announcement of regattas at Marblehead and race results, my antennae probed the air as cautiously as they had learned to probe the chalky fug of the Walley School. But the insults were subtler here: You could be snubbed and never know it.

Oil from the Coast Guard boats slicked the water near the dock, but none of us swimmers cared. I cannonballed off that dock a dozen times a day (my left leg still bears traces of the time the waves pushed me against a barnacle-

AMERICAN GIRL

crusted piling) and came up spitting gasoline. When the
dock palled, Ruthie, whom I had talked into joining, and I
would duck under the float at the side of the club, our heads
just above the water and our hands grasping its wooden
supports, to eavesdrop on the S. sisters, who were sunning
themselves just above us.

They were pretty, the younger in particular, and they
lounged on the float for hours, knitting intarsia sweaters
and rubbing Skol into each other's backs. Neither had gone
to college but, given their famous name, they couldn't be
expected to work either, and suitable husbands weren't
available in Bristol. So they drove around town in their little
car and sat on the porch of their little house and knitted
their little sweaters and waited. Perhaps their famous name
didn't really reverberate outside Rhode Island, but all Bristolians believed it did, and when a Bristol girl married a
New York millionaire there was talk that the S. girls might
meet the proper suitors—rich men anxious to blue their
bloodlines—at the reception. Alas, they did not, and went
on waiting, round and luscious in their Skol-soaked skins.

They were moist and she was dry. Nonetheless, the S.
sisters reminded me of Belle Bosworth, who skittered the
streets of Bristol with her parasol and her books, her lone-
liness frosting the air around her. On hot nights, when she
left her window open for what little breeze came from the
north, I could hear her typing in the room she rented at
Miss Munro's, a stone's throw from where I sat on the porch
glider. She was said to write poetry, and what the residents

of the country of the blue-eyed called "a good letter." I'd read one of them, sent my mother when she'd had a hysterectomy. After telling her how she envied her the hospital and the doctors and the nurses who were there to wait upon her hand and foot, Miss Bosworth said, "I am cold and desolate as a clam, and all the winds of Rhode Island and Providence Plantations are pressing against my window."

"That Belle Bosworth is a character, all right," my mother said, and slid the letter into her desk. It was embarrassing, she told me, but too good to throw away.

Yes, a character. All the old Yanks were characters, Ganny said. They couldn't help it. One Halloween night, when Ruthie and I were out looking for STOP signs to tip over, we saw Miss Bosworth butterflying down Hope Street, wearing a mask and trying to disappear into a crowd of roaming children. On summer afternoons, when the crowd down at Union Street had left for supper, she'd pick her way through the broken glass and the greasy bags to sit among the rocks and read till the sun went down. Once Diana saw a rat vault her lap. She didn't notice.

Her books were novels mostly, from the Rogers Free Library, but a few were schoolbooks. She was teaching herself the Romance languages and often, if I'd wandered down to watch the sun set, she'd ask me if I'd hold the book while she reeled off what she had memorized that day.

While she conjugated French verbs or counted one through ten in Italian, I'd check the text. "That's a devilish word," she'd say when corrected. "I hope I never have to use it." In me Miss Bosworth felt she'd found a kindred soul. I felt so too, and feared for my future.

But there were years to go before I might end up a spinster with skin as thin as crepe paper and dessicated veins, so I gave myself over to the long, green summer and the green light under the float, to the gentle slap of the water against the pilings and the click of the S. sisters' knitting needles and their murmured "Could you do my back?" and "Ooh, that sun is hot." And when Ruthie and I finally emerged, prune-skinned, there was the sleepy afternoon to look forward to, and the sight of Joseph Cotten coming in the door.

That is to say, he looked like Joseph Cotten. He was one of the summer people and soon to inherit $7,000,000 —from the poor side of the family. Their house on Monkeywrench Lane had a swimming pool, the only one in Bristol, and people said that when you swam underwater you could see the name of the estate spelled out in light bulbs.

His hair was fair and ridged like Joseph Cotten's, his eyes were blue like Joseph Cotten's, and his voice was the voice of Joseph Cotten, only flattened by St. Paul's and Yale. Ruthie stuck a recording of "I'll See You in My Dreams" on the old Victrola every time he entered the yacht club, but I doubt he noticed. I doubt he noticed much besides Linda.

Linda was the prettiest girl in Bristol. Her hair was long and dark, and so were her eyes, and in summer she toasted to the burnished brown of a coffee bean. If she could only get in with the right crowd, everybody said, Linda would marry well. That was why her parents were sending her to a junior college in Boston in the fall. Meanwhile she was spending the summer on the yacht club dock, rotating as regularly as a bird on a spit and looking at a glorious future out of her long sloe eyes.

Along about three o'clock she'd get up, shrug a long shirt over her two-piece swimsuit and saunter barefoot into the big downstairs room. "Anybody seen Teddy?" she'd drawl, the first words she'd said all day. Then she'd curl up in one of the big leather chairs, pull out an English Oval whose smoke she'd let curl up into her narrow nostrils, and stare at the doorway.

When Teddy/Joseph Cotten entered she'd leave as if to go to the ladies' room, then sneak upstairs to a small room that opened onto a large deck. The door was always locked—there was a cupboard bar up there—except for parties, but Joseph Cotten had acquired a key somehow. A few minutes later he followed.

For summer afternoon after summer afternoon the room was his and Linda's, and I longed for some adult to step out on deck, see the drawn curtains, and say "What's going on in there?" I'd never gotten away with anything, from telling lies to stealing change from my mother's purse, and I didn't want anybody else to, either.

Finally, on an afternoon when Ruthie and I were playing Ping-Pong and wondering, as usual, about what was going on upstairs and how far Linda was willing to go to get Teddy, high heels sounded in the club's foyer. In she came, an answered prayer. Linda's mother.

"Where's Linda?" she asked. "Upstairs with Teddy," I replied, keeping a straight face but waiting, as was Ruthie and everyone else in the room, for her to rush upstairs.

"Oh," she said and turning—click-click-click-click—left the yacht club.

My mother didn't believe me when I told her how Linda's mother, her old high school classmate, had deliberately left her daughter in a locked room with a boy. I must have misunderstood, or, rather, Linda's mother must have misunderstood me. "Don't you go around spreading stories like that, Mary Lee Cantwell," she said. "You've got too big an imagination."

But I didn't have too big an imagination. I'm not sure if I've ever had much of an imagination. I had eyes.

On the afternoon I handed round the egg-salad triangles I had seen the attention Bristol's locals paid each pearl that dropped from the Ferry crowd's lips. I had seen, too, the magnetic field that enclosed the rich as if it were a fence, and that I was able to pierce it only because I was carrying a tray. Linda could no more hope to open the gate and carry off one of those boys with the flattened *a*'s and the impenetrable courtesy than she could hope to climb Everest.

And neither, my antennae told me, could I.

Chapter Thirteen

If the front door of Guiteras Junior High School was ever opened, I do not know it. Its façade, which was grand and Grecian, faced a small pond called Silver Creek and the mansions on Poppasquash Point, but it presented a plain backside to the tarred parking lot and football field behind it. That's where we went in and out, boys through the door to the left, girls through the door to the right, and all of us monitored by the principal, who took no guff. Once he wiped the forbidden lipstick off a girl's mouth with his handkerchief; another time I saw him wrestle a boy to the ground. Nobody ever took offense, the boys in particular being flattered by the implication that we were all wild beasts.

Here we were neither little kids nor big kids. Guiteras was Limbo, a way station between elementary school, which was remembered as fun, and high school, which was assumed to be glorious. Guiteras was neither in nor out of town. Instead it was at the beginning of the Neck, a breezy, barren stretch where the oldest house in Bristol, the place the Congregationalists held their first meetings, was dying of neglect.

If I'd lived just a few blocks farther down toward the Ferry, I'd have been eligible for the school bus and its noisy camaraderie. As it was, I bicycled back and forth at least four miles a day, grateful for the solitude. There were two of me by now, or perhaps there always had been, the one who watched and the one who did, and we talked to each other constantly. "Wonder what Ralph Kinder's doing uptown at this time of day," I'd say as we biked past the post office. "Maybe he's got a package," the other Mary Lee would reply. It was a family trait, of course, this continual monitoring of other peoples' endlessly interesting lives. Our gossip never went beyond 232 Hope Street, but its rooms hummed with "Why do you suppose that light's on so late over at the Connerys?" and "Just saw a car turning into the Howes' driveway. Funny hour to have company, don't you think?"

Guiteras was the sieve in which future stenographers, domestics, and factory workers were separated out from future dentists and dermatologists. Now friendships were based not on the same neighborhood or the same church but on our parents' aspirations. Those of us who were slated for college or, at least, a genteel high school education— Ruthie, Joan, Jeanne, Anne, and I, for instance, and the best-mannered boys—took Ancient History and Latin, and littered our conversation with *"amo"* and *"cum"* and *"habemus."* Clearly, we would edit the Colt Memorial High

School yearbook someday, and have our positions on the honor rolls proclaimed in *The Bristol Phoenix*, and be the big cheeses at the Pastime on Friday nights. We knew it, too. We swaggered.

Suddenly our teachers became infinitely amusing to us, part of the scrapbooks we were unconsciously accumulating about our school days. Now we were old enough to have pasts, old enough to begin our sentences with "Do you remember when . . ." My favorite teacher was a small, round Italian who taught Latin and Ancient History. He found us infinitely amusing, too. His tongue was literally (he explored his lower right molars all day long) and figuratively forever in his cheek.

That I will go to my grave knowing that Hannibal crossed the Alps with elephants is because he once had the smallest boy in the class ride the back of the fattest boy down a row of desks masquerading as mountains. While Ruthie intoned Plato, he had me mime the shrewish Xanthippe turning a cold shoulder on the dying Socrates as the latter lay draped across a desk. Spurred by his invention, Ruthie, Joanie, and I formed a trio we called the three Neroinas and, wrapped in sheets and wearing our mothers' chenille bedroom slippers, sang a song we'd composed about why Rome fell. But despite this joyous introduction to the ancient world I remained dubious about anyone or anything that had come out of the Mediterranean. The day our Latin teacher said idly, "You know, you are all descendants of Roman soldiers," I raised my hand and claimed an exemption. "Most of my ancestors came from Ireland," I told him, "and I never heard tell of any Roman invasion there."

In grade school, physical education had consisted of standing next to one's desk touching fingers to toes while a teacher snapped "One-two! One-two!" At Guiteras we had a real gym instructor, a tall, terrifying woman in a bloomer suit and black support stockings, who strode through the shower room after class pulling back the curtains and peering into the cubicles to make sure that everyone was getting wet. "Under the shower, under the shower," she'd bark, while the girls from the back of town, for whom public nakedness was torture, cowered and covered their groins. One year everybody got plantar warts from the communal foot bath through which she insisted on herding us, and at lunchtime the tarred parking lot was thick with girls on crutches.

We played volleyball and girls' basketball, dullest of all games, in a dark and dreary gym lighted by high dirty windows. In warm weather we went outside and played softball on the football field. I lazed in left field, praying that nothing would come my way, mystified that anyone would care about hitting or catching that dumb ball. The sun burned my face, the grass made me sneeze, boredom had me dizzy.

At recess, where once we had played tag and marbles on the Common, we now stood on the parking lot in whispering clumps, eyeing the boys. Occasionally one of them would dart into our territory and grab a hat or a scarf. We'd scream.

Words like "cherry" floated over from their side to our side, and boasts that had the boys jittering like monkeys. "Had a date with Fat Teresa last night" was the most frequent.

Fat Teresa. I never saw Fat Teresa, but I didn't have to. I could imagine her. Her hair was black and oily, and her cheeks rose in mounds on either side of a button nose. Her hands were short and puffy and her breasts like elongated gourds, and her skirt was strained across a massive rump. The skin on her round, thick legs was stretched so they looked like sausages about to pop, and her feet were snuggled into little white socks and black A. S. Beck loafers. She was all I feared about sex incarnate, and I shivered at the picture my mind had made. When recess was over I bounded for the door, happy to be enclosed again in the safe, sinless scents of chalk and floor polish and old books.

Guiteras Junior High. Finally my teachers had taken on faces and I had taken on friends. But in my memory the years dissolve into one another and all that surfaces are film clips. They are always sepia-toned.

I see Diana, for instance, bouncing a small rubber ball at recess. She is wearing my tan coat, and her wrists and knees are rubbed raw by a November wind. Our coats were always alike, and when I outgrew mine it was automatically handed down to her. But Diana has gained inches on me without our parents' noticing, and my old coat is far too small for her.

She looks like the orphans in the movies, chilly, chapped, in ill-fitting clothes, and suddenly my heart feels fat in my chest. Because I see Diana day after day I don't see her at all. Now she is visible: fair-haired, with Papa's thick, dark eyebrows, and ankles like a bird's. Oblivious to the weather and to the sight she makes in that coat, she keeps on bouncing her ball, as blessedly unselfconscious as she was when she was a little girl poking out her fanny and raising her fists to "the great John L."

I see Ruthie and me on Poppasquash Point after school, pushing our bikes down a dirt road past a sign that reads NO TRESPASSERS. We are furtive because we fear arrest, and resentful that any part of Bristol should be off-limits. I can respect a neighbor's lawn and am proud that Papa drove a man from the Watchtower Society off ours—"I don't like what you people say about my church," he thundered—but I am furious that so few can prohibit entry to so many. The estates on Ferry Road don't faze me: They are simply houses with bigger than usual backyards. But Poppasquash has woods and deer and ponds that I will never see, and I cannot bear the proscription.

We don't go very far, only to Hey Bonnie Hall, the last but one of the great nineteenth-century mansions and soon to burn to the ground. No one enters it now but children looking for a mirror to break or a place on which to carve an initial, and peeking through a broken shutter on a tall

French window we glimpse books scattered on a mahogany floor. The house was grand once, and lovely, and it pains me that no ancestor of mine has ever lived in this place. I am jealous of those whose claim on Bristol is stronger than my own.

But it is an afternoon in a second-floor classroom that faces west toward Silver Creek and Poppasquash Point that I see most clearly. I remember the dialogue, too, and the slight choke of the little polka-dotted bow tie under the collar of my white blouse. We have art with a teacher named Miss Nerone once a week, and today I am the model, standing stiff and trying not to squint because the sun is low and shining in my eyes.

"Mary Lee," she says, "has a bony face, which means it has highlights and deep shadows. That makes it easy and interesting to draw. In fact, real artists often look for faces like Mary Lee's."

I am stunned, not because Miss Nerone says I am easy to draw—I know that already, having practiced self-portraits in front of the bedroom mirror—but because of her allusion to faces like mine. She has taken my cheekbones and the hollows beneath them out of Bristol and placed them elsewhere.

I know there is an elsewhere. Even so, elsewhere is not a place in which I have ever really imagined myself. But because Miss Nerone has set my kind of face in other parts of the world she has, somehow or other, set me there too.

I look out at the sun, which is dipping its fingers into Bristol Harbor, and I am so excited I can hardly hold the pose.

"White lace. I think. Mary Lee." Miss Nerone was visualizing the dress I would wear the day I went down the aisle of St. Mary's Church to marry—whom? Someone, Miss Nerone said, I have yet to meet, but whom I will meet, as I will meet so many other exciting people once I get out of Bristol. Miss Nerone loves Bristol. There is no town like Bristol. But it is not the *world*. Peggy Nerone, Margaret Frances Nerone, art supervisor for the public schools of Bristol, Rhode Island, spoke in italics.

Miss Nerone's eyes were big and green and slightly popped (after her sister saw *Now Voyager* she said, "Bette Davis was the dead spit of Peggy. I've never seen her look so bad"), and one front tooth curtsied across the other. She was said to be New Yorkish, what with getting her clothes there and being the only person in town who dared a Kelly-green coat and a hat with a feather that stabbed the sky, and thought nothing of running up to Boston for a show. She was always running, one way or another, and the freckles on the back of her legs made them look perpetually mud-splashed. "Ompen the window!" she'd say huskily when she entered a classroom. "Hand me an ampron!" when she bustled about her tiny kitchen. Besides not looking like anybody else in Bristol, she didn't sound like anybody else either.

MARY CANTWELL

Miss Nerone lived on Church Street, nestled under the eaves of a tall, thin house. The ceilings of her apartment slanted and those windows that weren't close to the floor were set in dormers. All of them wore wooden shutters instead of curtains. Where the light wasn't green it was amber, and together they cast what I now recognize as a Pre-Raphaelite shimmer over the Victorian furniture, the crammed bookcases, the funny old prints, and the framed autograph of Eamon de Valera. "Welcome to my garret," she said to those who made the three-flight climb up the back stairs. "Mind the door!"

Years of students made that climb and had their futures prophesied by Peggy Nerone. "If you'll just get out of Bristol you can be . . . you can be . . . you can be." Few of them ever did, and then she said "if only . . . if only . . . if only." The abilities she saw in us, realized or not, she saw forever. None of Miss Nerone's pets were ever failures. It was just that they'd postponed success.

Peggy Nerone, whom I was never to call by her first name, and Papa were pals. Sometimes they walked uptown together, talking about New York and Graham Greene and William Butler Yeats and the new movies, both of them starved for a certain kind of conversation that Papa called "smart talk." He was pleased when, on a spring evening during my last term at Guiteras Junior High, I made the climb to the garret for the first time. Miss Nerone had invited me for dinner, and here, maybe, was the world in which I'd like to live someday.

AMERICAN GIRL

I was fussy about clothes by now, and tortured my hair with bobby pins and kid curlers and rag rollers, and more than once my father had chastised me for looking too long into the mirror. That's why I remember so well what I was wearing: a flowered rayon jumper, all greens and yellows with a splash of magenta, over a long-sleeved white blouse. I was also wearing my retainer, a semicircle of wire attached to a pink plastic plate over which I was supposed to position my lower jaw. It was the last stage in seven years of nonstop orthodontia.

We had sherry before the consommé, the candles flickered in the May night, and I recall being pleased at how well I was doing: my back straight, my left forearm invisible and my soup spoon skimming away from, not toward, me. Miss Nerone told me to be sure to read James Stephens's *Crock of Gold*, and that I must, I really must, ask Papa to take me to the Gardner Museum and to the Ballet Russe de Monte Carlo when it came to Boston. The world was expanding as she spoke, and so was I.

Then it happened. After the roast chicken and the peas and the vanilla ice cream, I looked for the plastic retainer presumably hidden in my lap. It wasn't there. How could I face my parents, who had spent a fortune for this hardware? There was nothing for it but to ask Miss Nerone to help me look for the darn thing.

Together we crawled about the rug searching for the retainer which, out of my mouth, looked like an especially hideous set of dentures. Then I remembered. Before we'd sat down at the small walnut table I had palmed the retainer and slid it into my jumper pocket.

By now my eyes were wet and my face red and my back damp. "It's in my pocket," I said, still staring at the floor.

"Only Mary Lee Cantwell would have her hostess on her hands and knees," Miss Nerone crowed, and sent me home a queen.

That summer Miss Nerone roped Ruthie and me into the Bristol Community Theater. Bristol hadn't had a little theater since Aida Connery's glory days, when she'd been Butterfly in *H.M.S. Pinafore* and Peg in *Peg O' My Heart*. Instead we had the Rotary Club Minstrel, for which Ganny's cousin, Emma Rounds, played the piano and Miss Nerone did the makeup. But Bristol had what my mother described—in a lemon-juice voice—as "an arty crowd" and it clamored for something more than blackface and straw hats. That was why Ruthie and I who, hanging on her every word, walked Miss Nerone home whenever she taught at Guiteras, found ourselves one night sitting timidly in a corner of a smoke-filled room above the Y.M.C.A.

Some of the arty crowd were new to Bristol and some were what my mother called sissy, but all of them were people I'd seen traipsing about town and in and out of the Pastime behaving just like everybody else. Here, though, they were transformed.

They perched on tables, rather than on the Y's folding chairs, swinging their legs (if they weren't crossed) and taking deep drags on their cigarettes. They talked fast, too, more often out of the side than out of the center of their mouths, and their consonants rang like steel. Ruthie and I didn't catch their references, nor did we get their jokes, but I was certain we were listening to smart talk.

Kitty Foyle was to be the first production, and having found a Kitty (the prettiest girl in the senior class at Colt Memorial High School) the arty crowd was looking around for a Veronica Gladwyn, the rich boy's snooty fiancée. "There she is, right over there!" the smartest talker—a man whose hands waved like palm fronds—exclaimed, and pointed at me, bony-faced beyond my fourteen years.

On the evening of the performance, in the same dirty-windowed gymnasium in which I'd played girls' basketball, Miss Nerone sank my cheeks with rouge, dimmed my skin with powder and painted my lips into Katharine Hepburn's downturn. My costume was a broad-shouldered black crepe dress loaned by my stage mother, and black suede pumps loaned by my real mother, and when I stood waiting in the wings with the rest of the cast, all of us in paint and powder and borrowed clothes and sheepish smiles, I felt myself one of a company of players, their age and their peer. Then the house lighs dimmed and Eddy Duchin's recording of "Love Walked In" troubled the hush—sad and sonorous and the smartest talk I'd ever heard.

It sounded like New York, the New York that Miss Nerone talked about when she came home from her summers working in Saks Fifth Avenue's handbag department. A place where you could see Ginger Rogers tapping an impatient toe at a glove counter (Miss Nerone had) and skyscrapers pierced clouds and something called a shuttle burrowed between Times Square, where the lights were, and Grand Central, where the *Yankee Clipper* pulled in puffing.

But no matter how Miss Nerone's green eyes glowed in the telling, nobody at 232 Hope Street, except for Papa, would have dreamed of living in a world where laundry dripped into bathtubs instead of grass, and one slept on sheets that had never known sun.

My mother had gone to New York several times, and kept in the desk a photograph, framed in fake red plush, of her and Papa sitting at a table in Billy Rose's Diamond Horseshoe. Beside Esther's bed was a picture of herself and Agnes, one of the girls from the shop, at the World's Fair. And, of course, there was that other trip, when she, along with all the other fans, pushed and shoved to see Rudy in his coffin. Gampa, too, had been to New York, on its outskirts anyway, when he and Ralph Kinder would zoom along the Merritt Parkway to see how fast they could get from Bristol to there and back. Still, no amount of shows, nightclubs, neon signs, and puffing camels could make up for the crowds, the dirt, and the heat. "You don't get a breeze like this in New York," Bristol said when the harbor flashed little white ruffles. "They say the prices in New York are something terrible. . . ." "I bet you don't get lobster like this in New York."

Eddy Duchin went on picking out the melody, each

note clean and firm and somber. The music sounded like what you got out of Bristol for, but what that was I couldn't have said. New York was as good a term as any, if by it you meant something that was more an idea than a place.

Papa, Gampa, Ganny, Esther, and Diana were out front, along with Mother, who was just sliding into her seat. A few minutes earlier she'd sneaked backstage to see how I looked in the black crepe dress and the high-heeled shoes. Side by side we stood, staring into the full-length mirror propped against a wall, and for once there were no proscriptions about admiring oneself.

My eyes were brown to her blue; my head topped hers by a good three inches. But we had the same broad cheekbones and the same broad shoulders. I would never be as pretty as my mother, but I had inherited enough of her to be handsome. "Boy!" I thought to myself. "I look like New York."

Chapter Fourteen

A few years ago, sitting in a cab that was going up Madison Avenue and staring through the rain at the umbrellas and puddles and the shops that sold French bags and Italian shoes and English chintzes, it suddenly occurred to me that I was happy. But why? It was the way the cab smelled.

The previous passenger had been wearing shaving lotion, something ordinary like Old Spice or Aramis, and to sniff that scent was to be in the glider on the second-floor porch of 232 Hope Street, with a boy whose whose shirt smelled of starch and fresh air and whose young, flushed face smelled of his older brother's aftershave. He was the boy I had seen at the Pastime Theater when I was eleven or so, and for all the time I was in that cab he was in it too.

He had dark wiry hair and a thin wide mouth, and all that was even slightly exceptional about him were his eyes, which were very blue. His eyes were what I noticed the night I looked along the row at the Pastime. I don't know what it was he noticed about me.

AMERICAN GIRL

Who was he? I had never seen him at the Pastime before, nor at Buffington's Drugstore, nor at church. I was pretty sure he wasn't one of the summer people because it was in winter that I had seen him; and he didn't go to St. Mary's, the Congregational Church (I asked Joanie) or St. Michael's (I asked Anne).

I looked for him at Alger's Newsstand and at the library, and on Friday nights when I went to the Pastime my eyes were searchlights sweeping the lobby and the aisles. But I didn't find him for over a year, and when I did it was in the tarred parking lot of Guiteras Junior High.

It was the first day of school and he was standing alone, sliding quick looks in my direction. He lived up the Neck, somebody said, miles away from 232 Hope Street, and had just graduated from St. Mary's Parochial School. No wonder he'd been invisible.

His name was Norman, and he was entering the ninth grade. I was just entering the seventh. When he left Guiteras I would be just moving into the eighth, whereas he would have gone on to the greater glory that was Colt Memorial High School. By the time I got there he'd have gone out with lots of girls, maybe even kissed a few. But at least I'd have a year during which we'd be passing each other in the hallways, hanging around the same parking lot, sharing the same auditorium.

It would have been enough to go on staring, to glimpse him as he traveled the corridors, to sit in the seat that had been his when he left for his next class. But he kept on sliding those quick looks, and the boys on the school bus howled and stroked their index fingers and chanted "Normie likes Mary Lee-ee! Normie likes Mary Lee-ee!" Still, we never spoke.

There was a little ritual we schoolkids practiced every June: mock terror when the report cards were handed out. Suppose we hadn't passed? But of course we passed. Only odd kids with streaming noses and wet lips weren't promoted. So I was stunned when the whispering began on the girls' side of the parking lot. Norman, cocky Norman, would have to repeat ninth grade.

For a minute I fell out of love, and then, laboriously, I fell back in. Norman was moody, unpredictable, untameable. He was, in fact, the lover for whom Ruthie and I cried at the foot of Union Street. "Heathcliff," we'd call into the wrinkling water and the setting sun. "Where are you, Heathcliff?" Heathcliff would not have given a fig for not passing ninth grade.

Another year with Norman: Ruthie said it was fate. The following fall he started drifting away from the boys with whom he stood at recess. Each day he drifted a little farther until, finally, he ended up on the girls' side. "Saw you up on the Common, Tuesday," he'd say, and "Bet you *live* at the library."

Standing so close to him made me nervous. "I didn't see *you*," I'd reply, and "I do *not*."

Ruthie, Joanie, Jeanne, and Anne would giggle, and

back to the boys' side he'd saunter. The boys would cuff his arms or try to trip him; I'd turn away, pleasure spreading through me like warm milk.

Sometimes he walked me home, veering off to kick a horse chestnut or jump for a dangling leaf, then homing back to my side. We seldom talked. If we had, I might have said "What was it about me?" I might even have said "I think it was your eyes."

No, I wouldn't have. I would have chattered about anything in the world but love, and when, years later, he asked me to say the word—just say the word—the "*l*" stuck to my tongue.

Every Saturday afternoon I went to confession, kneeling in a golden oak box and scraping my mind for sins. "I got mad at my sister three times, Father, and twice I disobeyed my mother." Taking communion on Sunday meant being visible to everyone in church, and I wanted Norman to see me, pretty in my reefer and beret and transfigured by piety. He no longer went to the eleven o'clock mass with his family—that they went to that service was another reason I'd never seen him until that night at the Pastime—but took the bus downtown to sit alone across the aisle from us at the nine o'clock. When I left the communion rail, my mouth closed primly over the wafter, I'd sneak a glance toward his pew. If he was there, I sank to the kneeler and buried my face in my hands. In theory I was praying, but in fact I was smiling, and the heat from my cheeks was warming my fingers. "Forgive your sister," Papa would say when I snarled at Diana or refused her a game of slapjack. "She's in love."

"Did Hotlips walk you home from school today?" he'd ask over supper. Norman played the trumpet. I kept my own lips shut when Papa teased, but happiness curled them at the corners. Someday Norman was going to kiss them, the first boy who ever did, but I could wait. Because what I really wanted was to pass right into him.

I had never been lonely before, even when nobody at school liked me. I had always had myself to talk to. But I wasn't enough for me anymore. Now when I walked down Union Street after an evening up at Ruthie's, the scent of salt and privet, which I had loved, made me desolate instead. I peered into the Tingleys' and Miss Munro's lighted windows and believed myself to be irrevocably outside, destined, like Belle Bosworth, to butterfly down Hope Street forever. Still, desolation was exciting. "Alone, alone," I chanted, and marveled at the sound the words made, like a bell tolling. Once in a while I kept on walking, right down to where the water lapped, black and oily in the dark. Rats whispered among the rocks, and the damp curled my hair. "She walks in beauty like the night," I breathed, and assigned the words to me.

Spring arrived, the last spring that Norman would be at Guiteras Junior High. He had passed. The horse chestnuts in front of 232 Hope Street were strung with candles;

the linden trees in front of Colt Memorial loosed their scent; when the rain fell in late afternoon it felt like a sponge full of warm water was being squeezed over my head. And Norman, at last, picked up the family telephone and asked for four-six-one.

My mother washed my hair in the afternoon while I hung my head over the side of the bathtub, and gave it a chamomile rinse. I put on my best dress, a shadow-plaided pink-and-white cotton, white socks, and my Bass Weejuns, and replaced my silver barrette with a maroon grosgrain ribbon.

Breathless in my perfection I went downstairs so Ganny, Gampa, and Esther could look me over, then trotted back upstairs so Mother, Papa, and Diana could have their turn. "See he brings you straight home afterward," my mother said, and retied the bow in my hair. When the doorbell rang I was reluctant to answer; reluctant to leave this room and Diana in her long braids and Mother taking off her apron and Papa pushing up the knot on his loosened tie and all of them smiling at Mary Lee, who was about to cast off from the dock.

It was still daylight, which meant that everyone could see us when we walked uptown. So when we got to Court Street I made him walk ahead of me so that the guys who hung around the front of the Y.M.C.A. and had something to say about everyone who passed wouldn't realize we were together.

MARY CANTWELL

Once past the Y and across State Street Norman stopped and, turning, waited until I caught up. Then we linked hands for the first time, and walked under the linden trees up to Bradford Street. We were heading, of course, for the Friday night show at the Pastime Theater.

Chapter Fifteen

Where I live now, close to the Hudson, the air smells of iodine, and seagulls dive into the piles of debris heaped beside the docks. By most people's standards it's a desolate area, but not by mine. The water and the gulls remind me of Bristol, and I am as at home here as I can ever be in New York. There's one thing that's bothersome, though. The traffic. I can never get away from the whine of traffic.

If I interrupt this narrative, it is because I want to celebrate a silence, a silence I can't find even in Bristol anymore. In my childhood, Bristol was noisy only with winds and birds and people's voices and lawn mowers and waves lapping and factory whistles hooting and pins scattering at the bowling alley. Except on Saturdays, when uptown was clogged with cars unloading passengers at the library or Buffington's or one of about twelve stores, ten cars heading south in five minutes were enough to make Ganny say "They're going to have a regular traffic jam down by the Mount Hope Bridge."

A car going through town late at night was reason to rush to the window. What, short of an emergency, could bring anyone out of the road after eleven o'clock? A car suddenly braking in front of the house had my mother saying "Must be one of those crazy New York drivers."

Families had cars, of course. They used them to go to Providence, and if they lived up the Neck or down the Ferry they used them to go to church on Sundays. On the night of the Junior Prom or the Senior Reception at Colt Memorial High they lent them to their sons; and the sons of families that didn't have cars were frantic until they found a friend with whom to double-date, because one couldn't ask a girl to trail her evening gown through town. But most of the time Bristolians walked. Walking was economical; it was healthful; and, most important, it was virtuous. To ride when you could walk betrayed a kind of moral sloth.

On Thanksgiving Day when we were small Diana and I walked toward the Ferry with Esther, so as to work up an appetite for the turkey. Esther couldn't make anything but penuche, so nobody expected her in the kitchen, and setting the table was Gampa's job because he'd learned from his brother, the one who'd owned the Warren Hotel, how to fold napkins into fancy shapes. So Esther was free, as she was always free, to be our playmate. She was also free of ever having to be called "aunt." From the beginning Diana, myself, and Miss Hot-Cha, Miss Charleston (she taught us how, hands grasping the back of a chair), Miss-Five-Foot-Two-Eyes-of-Blue were the same age.

Off we'd go, scuffling through the leaves and taking deep breaths—Esther believed that salt air was good for the lungs and salt water good for the skin, which was why hives and rashes always had us standing neck-deep in Bristol Harbor—and exchanging good mornings with other Bristolians out to work up an appetite. Usually there were one or two boats tacking their way about the harbor, somebody out for a last sail before winter set in.

Our eyes on the harbor, Diana and I pretended not to notice when Esther scooted ahead of us to hide behind a tree. Dutifully we screamed when she leaped out, then on we'd go. When we got to the yellow caution light suspended above the intersection of Hope and Wood Street she'd say "Getting hungry, girls?" and not waiting for an answer turn back, the ritual complete.

Once past the caution light one was down the Ferry, and no longer on a walk but taking a hike. A hike meant continuing down the worn, leaf-carpeted path on the west side of Ferry Road (the right side was grassy and pathless and on higher ground) past a house with two porcelain cats on its roof, a Gothick cottage and, beyond a gatehouse, the rhododendron-screened summer residence of a rich Providence family, all of whom had long teeth and carrot-colored hair.

No matter how bright the sun or how warm the day the air was damp and cool at the beginning of the Ferry. Moisture dropped from the dense evergreens and the leaf mold smelled like melancholy. Squirrels made sudden darts up trees and down stone walls. There were no passersby, and the houses were still and secretive.

Stillest of all was a house called Blithewold, whose owners were seldom, if ever, there. Blithewold was separated from the path only by knee-high stone walls between whose posts swung long, loose chains. Even so, no intruder ever strolled its thirty-three acres or sheltered in the shade of its copper beech or its sequoia, the tallest for thousands of miles, or sat in its tiny gazebo. No guards were needed to keep the stranger off the grass; the house itself did that.

Sprawled insolently on the lawn, its white stucco shining in the sun, it turned blind windows on the world, and I, eating my hiker's apple on the low wall, trembled lest, sensing my presence, it told me to get up. Every once in a while in Bristol, money, old money, rose up and hit you in the face. Sometimes it was in the form of a sentence—"But everyone we *want* to know about it will be there," a friend from the yacht club said when I asked if her debut would be reported in the *Providence Journal.* Sometimes it was in the form of a locked and silent house.

Past Blithewold the trees thinned and hills rolled and crouched behind them, invisible from the road, were St. Joseph's Seminary, which sent St. Mary's its summer priests, and the Convent of St. Dorothy, home to an order of Portuguese nuns of whom nobody ever saw hide nor hair. Behind St. Joseph's a large crucifix reached by a long flight of stone steps brooded over the harbor. For several Good Friday's Ruthie and I knelt on those steps for the long hours from noon to three o'clock when the sky darkened and the heavens split and Jesus gave up his spirit. But I could summon no more religiosity there than I could in the attic during the days before my First Communion, when I waited among the chamber pots for God to send me a sign. There was no room in this spartan landscape for votive lights and chasubles and bleeding hearts. The very town looked Protestant.

As one neared the end of the Ferry the road forked, and Narragansett Bay blazed blue. To the right was the entrance to the Mount Hope Bridge; to the left a short stretch of road that ended in a rocky shore. Here old men fished for flounder while the occasional car sped overhead across the bridge, and the occasional suicide tumbled from the bridge railings. Usually they went over without a sound, but a woman from Barrington, who had traveled hell-for-leather down Hope Street to make the plunge, screamed when she hit the air. Everybody said she had probably changed her mind the minute her foot left the railing.

Beyond the shore, crumbling cliffs edged the meadows in which cows browsed and dropped the flops that had Ruthie and me uttering warning cries and, all too often, a disgusted "Ugh." We wandered the meadows every spring and fall looking for arrowheads and striking romantic poses; and once a friend spent the night in that lonely place. At least that is what we think she did the time she ran away from home. We never asked, afraid the answer might involve a boy and a precocity we perceived as dirty. Neither did her mother, who feared her daughter's flat blue eyes. So we all chose to imagine her in the meadows, sitting against a tree, shivering in the dark, while cows lowed and cars hummed on the bridge and Indians pussyfooted along the paths that would take them to Mount Hope and Philip's longhouse.

We never walked down the Ferry in winter. The meadows were sodden, and the wind that came off Narrgansett Bay was wet and cold as an icicle. Instead we walked north, toward the Neck and, if it had snowed, Fort Hill, where Lafayette had stamped about and slept and ate and which he abandoned when the harbor froze and locked the town.

Snow must have fallen in Bristol by day as well as by night, but it is always in the dark that I see the flakes, whirling ghostlike around the streetlights or dropping past them straight as needles. Down into the front hall Diana and I would creep, to open the door and watch snow blanket the bushes and the lawn and the empty roadway, and listen to its curious hiss. In the morning we awoke to deep drifts and iced trees and the scrape of Gampa's shovel on the sidewalk.

Come afternoon, we bellyflopped down Fort Hill, me on the bottom because I was the older, one hand steering our Yankee Flyer, the other over my mouth so a spill wouldn't lay waste to years of orthodontia, the two of us diving straight into the western sun. It was low in the sky by three o'clock, and orange, and the shadows in the snow were blue. By the time we left the hill for the long walk home, everything around us was white or gray or black.

Because no Bristolian would dream of turning on the electricity while it was still light out, the houses were as desolate as the streaming gutters. The windows in some were chinked with newspaper and fogged with the torrid heat from kerosene stoves whose pipes had been tunneled into sealed fireplaces. Bristol was a hard place for the elderly to be in winter, less because it was cold than because the damp was cruel to old bones. Still, I never heard of anyone leaving town. Old bones stayed indoors with Ma Perkins and her handyman, Shuffle, and got their groceries delivered and didn't show their faces until the end of March, when the backyards were mud and the milk had stopped freezing and forcing the cream out of the tops of the bottles.

As I got older Fort Hill palled, and the Yankee Flyer became Diana's alone. Now Ruthie, Joanie, Jeanne, Anne, and I, our ice skates tied together and hanging around our necks, hiked every Saturday to Collins Pond, to skate with the boys we knew from birthday parties and Girl Scouts. But I, the first of us to have an official boyfriend, skated mostly with Norman. Sometimes he stuck his bare hand into my mitten, and our entangled fingers became slick with sweat. He couldn't quite look in my eyes then, nor I in his.

Collins Pond was in a hollow behind a two-room schoolhouse, and had narrow, reed-bordered tributaries that meandered eastward toward St. Mary's Cemetery, where Ganny's family slept row on row. One could travel the tributaries single file until they narrowed too much even for a blade, and whenever I skated into the reeds I felt as if I

were slipping through centuries. But not into Bristol's past.
Miss Nerone had shown the class a print of Brueghel's
Woodchoppers, and it was into that still, serene landscape I
was skating.

Dressed in caps, scarves, mittens, peajackets, snow
pants, and two or three pairs of socks apiece, we bumbled
up and down the pond, stumbling over our own and everyone else's blades and frequently crashing to the ice. And
just as the woodchoppers are fixed on canvas so we are fixed
on my mind, to go on bumbling and stumbling and crashing
until the projector shuts down.

Across the road from Collins Pond two bronze bulls,
snorting and stamping on their marble pedestals, proclaimed the entrance to Colt Farm, Private Property, Public
Welcome.

S. Pomeroy Colt, the man who inflated the rubber
works, had had a good time with his money. He ran a road
around the farm's perimeter, threw a bridge over an inlet
called Mill Gut, and set facsimilies of the Venus de Milo
and the Discus Thrower on its buttresses. The Jersey cows
he named after his girlfriends were housed in a tile-roofed
stone barn, and a big, shingled casino in which he gave
glorious luncheons boasted a statue of Silenus holding a
goatskin purse that spurted milk punch.

By the time I came along, S. Pomeroy, his girlfriends,
his luncheon guests, and his cows were dead, the casino
was in ruins and Silenus had disappeared. But the barn sat
solid and substantial on a sea of grass, and the bronze dog

S. Pomeroy had set on a pudding stone near a narrow beach still stared at Narragansett Bay.

The dog was death to the touch but so lifelike to look at that I half-believed it had watched the boats that ran along this pebbly shore during Prohibition. If it had, it might have seen my grandfather among the Bristolians who stood ankle-deep in the purling water, passing the cases from hand to hand while the moon sailed overhead. Or so I had heard. But I couldn't ask Gampa if the story was true, because he'd have been as embarrassed by the question as he was by his granddaughters having seen him the night he was escorted home from the Hurricane Bar. Nor could I ask Ganny, because any talk of liquor had her frowning, or my mother, because she'd say "Where did you ever hear such a thing?" and be cross at suppertime. But I believed it. Even when he was walking Judy uptown on the end of her clothesline leash, with his shirt open at the neck and his pants flapping about his skinny legs, Gampa had the air of a Dapper Dan. I could see him in that purling water, oh yes, with the moon shining on his white hair and a cigarette in the corner of his mouth.

Before there had been any Colts or cows or bronze bulls or bootleggers, however, there had been the poorhouse. It was still up there, white as a skull, with three rows of hollow eyes that stared at North Burial Ground. To explore it one had to hazard a deceptively grass-filled ditch and a barrier of nettles, but they weren't what kept the poorhouse unviolated. Bleached and bare and bony, it evoked what lay beneath the burying ground's old slate markers and the flags that waved cheerily on veterans' graves.

"I shall end up in the poorhouse," Ganny would say whenever she looked into her change purse, and meant it. She remembered when people really did: old Yanks and a few old Irish, some of them dirty and some of them clean, some of them well-mannered and some of them know-nothings, and all of them with faded blue eyes.

Beyond the poorhouse a long straight road arrowed through a double file of maple trees under which the Portuguese and Italian families who lived in the three-deckers off Wood Street picnicked in summer while their children swam off the flat gray shingle known as the Town Beach. The children shrieked and the parents shouted, but the cars parked on the grass slumbered until it was time to pack up the kids and the coolers and the leftover *chourice* and go home.

Sunday afternoon was our time at Colt Farm, when Ruthie, Joanie, Jeannie, and I walked the entire perimeter, stopping only to take snapshots of one another, our faces turned to the wind so we could display our profiles and our skirts plastered against our lean thighs.

We walked through air that was as silver as the bay, following the road that led us past the poorhouse and through the file of trees and over the bridge to the head of the harbor.

We passed the little hill on which my mother had sat with a beau for a photograph, toothy and pretty, her arms

curved around her silk-stockinged legs and her feet long
and narrow in her T-strapped shoes. Uncle John had posed
for a picture here, too, handsome and a bit flashy in his
two-toned wingtips, and companioned by a girl in a cloche
hat and skimpy jersey dress.

We passed S. Pomeroy's stone barn, and families clam-
ming in the shallow, polluted water and, in the last stretch,
a peculiar building called the Castle, stuccoed and turreted
and ugly. And when, abruptly, we were out on Hope Street
again we saw Guiteras Junior High just down the road and
moaned.

We walked, no matter how late the hour or how long
the distance from here to there. We walked down the Ferry
and up the Neck, along the Back Road and across the Common, down Thames Street, where spinning mills thrummed
and spilled their dyes into the harbor, and up Tanyard Lane
where in spring some funny, fleshy plants poked what look
like penises out of pale-green leaves and made us blush and
titter.

We walked along Wood Street, past U. S. Rubber with
its red-brick archway, past cobblers' shops and dimly lit
stores that sold bacalao and olive oil, past St. Mary's Parochial School and St. Mary's Church and the convent for
the Sisters of Mercy and the old town graveyard, and past
the dingy bar in whose backroom a rich, high-nosed parish-
ioner of St. Michael's held court among the town layabouts
every Sunday after church.

We walked through salt air and burnt-rubber air, under

skies that were clotted with clouds or gray as pewter or as hard and blue as Canton ware. We walked at night when there wasn't another soul on the street and the trees sighed and dipped their heads and the bushes shuddered in the dark. We walked if it rained and we walked if it snowed and we walked if whitecaps presaged a squall. When a hurricane came up, and seventeen miles of flooded roads and downed trees lay between the Tingley boys' father and home, he did what any Bristolian would have done. He walked.

Chapter Sixteen

Finally it had arrived: my first day at Colt Memorial High School. My blooming.

I would go to football and basketball games, no longer a shy spectator unsure of my place in the crowd but an acquaintance of the guys on the team, a friend of the cheerleaders. I would see my name in *The Bristol Phoenix* when I made the honor roll, and on Friday nights I would swagger down the aisle of the Pastime Theater because this was my territory now. And when the crowds gathered on a May night to watch the Tonys in their white dinner jackets and the Annas in pastel tulle arriving for the Junior Prom, they would see me too. Mary Lee Cantwell, the dead spit (I thought) of Gene Tierney.

When I was six or so Diana and I—she in a checked cotton dress that hugged her cheerful plumpness and I in an eyelet-edged gingham that hung off my bony shoulders—stood on the marble steps of the high school, along with thirty other females of assorted sizes and shapes.

We were participants in a pageant celebrating 300 years of Rhode Island, and all the costumes, all but the two Puritan get-ups, came from Bristol attics.

A photographer from the *Phoenix* took our picture, and Papa ordered two copies: one for me and one for Di for when we grew up. I love to look at it, not simply because I know so many of the faces—Miss Nerone is there, and Miss Hill, two of the four beautiful sisters who used to ride their horses in the Fourth of July parade, and the leader of my Girl Scout Mariners troop—but because it shows so clearly the astonishment that was Colt Memorial High.

Colt Memorial High School was S. Pomeroy Colt's tribute to his mother, Theodora, and he had brought to it the same passion for the ancient world that had informed his improvements to Colt Farm. In the first place, the school was a veritable temple of learning, being completely faced with marble, its windows set in bronze.

On either side of the marble walkway stood a bronze boy and a bronze girl. He wore a few odds and ends of drapery; she wore a chiton and was holding a book. Hair bound in a fillet, her nose straight as a die, she looked like my mother, who might have modeled for Praxiteles.

The walkway led to marble steps that in turn led to a massive mahogany front door framed by Corinthian columns and enormous bronze lanterns. To the left of the entrance was a big block of marble supporting beasts and men in bloody combat; Rodin's *Naked Eve* would have graced the front lawn had not the School Committee of 1909 demurred. To walk in the front door of Colt Memorial High School was, in theory if not in fact, to set foot on Parnassus.

So here I am, on a warm day in early September, coming down the steps of 232 Hope Street in the blue-and-white striped dress that, outgrown or not, is my lucky charm for every first day of school. The horse chestnuts are just beginning to litter the sidewalk, and I—sniffing the air, tossing my pageboy—am in full gallop.

On this as on every schoolday for the next three years a flat blue purse that closes with two red Bakelite stars is balanced on top of the notebooks cradled in my left arm. All it will ever hold is a comb, a handkerchief, small change, and a tube of Chen Yu lipstick, but to go out without it is inconceivable. Ruthie, Joanie, Jeanne, and Anne also carry such purses, shielding their contents from the boys when they lift the flaps, implying that they cache female secrets. Sanitary napkins, say, and the attendant safety pins.

Behind me, Mother is sitting down for her second cup of coffee, an English Oval in her left hand and relief written all over her face. We are out of the house, all of us, and the silence is settling over her shoulders as lightly as a swansdown cloak. We wear her out, we Cantwells.

Downstairs Ganny is punching pillows and yanking sheets, and if she can talk Gampa into hauling it out to the clothesline for her, she'll probably go out to the backyard and beat Esther's bedroom rug. It is wonderful to see Ganny at work. Unable to bend, she washes the kitchen floor by pushing the rag around with her foot. When she is making a pie she tosses the pastry as if it were pizza dough. "Get that hound out from underfoot," she calls to Gampa as she perambulates the house. "Tom, why don't you take that dang dog out for a walk?" Meanwhile he, bored and restless, is skimming the newspaper or dipping into the only book he ever reads. It is Mary Lasswell's *Suds in Your Eye*, picked up once or twice a week, and makes him laugh till his nose runs.

Ahead of me, uptown is shaking itself out of sleep. Newman's Grocery is gone, but the grumpy old man from whom I used to buy foreign stamps for my album, ten per glassine envelope, is sweeping the sidewalk in front of his variety store. I bob my head in his direction, a queen in a glass coach, but he is sour and saurian as ever. Miss Norah Sullavan of The Bluebird Shoppe is sweeping her sidewalk, too, the secrets of every female bulge, sag, and varicosity in the country of the blue-eyed safe beneath her massive corset.

Across the street from the Bluebird, Ralph Kinder, the florist, is wiring the stems for the roses in today's first coffin blanket. If Ganny succeeds in getting Gampa out of the house, he'll be sitting at Kinder's in an hour or so, slapping his knee while Ralph skewers the passersby. If anyone comes in the shop, he'll show them Judy's gallstones, which he keeps in a pocket of his vest. "Did I ever show you what my little dog had in her?" he'll ask. He probably has, but the person will look anyway. That Gampa is crazy about Judy is well known in our part of town.

Next to Kinder Florists, the woman who runs the beauty

parlor where Mother gets her semiannual permanent has the front door open to let the air in; but the Women's Exchange will stay shut until noon. The tarnished spoons and brass candlesticks and dusty Limoges in its window are testament to a hundred Bristol weddings. Its proprietor, a pillar of St. Michael's Church, is testament to Bristol's years in the slave trade, being both black and a member of the town's most prominent family.

Beyond the Solders' and Sailors' Monument and the police station, Alger's Newsstand is doing a brisk trade in *The Providence Journal* and *The Bristol Phoenix*, and the latter's editor is dashing into the post office for the first mail. A small, skinny man with a toothbrush mustache, he is always dashing—scooping up the news, I suppose—and I am proud when he stops to tip his hat and croon "Goo-oo-ood morning, Mary Lee!"

The regulars for morning coffee at Buffington's have taken their places at the marble counter, but the awnings aren't yet down at Eisenstadt's Dry Goods. Thank heaven the sidewalk in front of the Y is still free of the boys who'll be there later, cracking wise.

Once across State Street I am part of the crowd converging on Colt High. If Bristol were still the town I have created out of Ganny's stories, the students would look like George Gibb and Emily Webb or, closer to home, my mother in her youth. The actuality, however, is Dolores Canario and Anthony Guglielmo. How can I see the Bristol I want to see, the Bristol where Indians stalked Mount Hope and George Washington paraded down Hope Street and Ganny, in her best dress and high-topped shoes, stood weeping at her mother's grave, when the town has taken on so Neapolitan an air?

And yet I can, because by now I have double vision. I have listened so long to Ganny's stories and spent so many hours studying the pictures in her copy of *The 1903 Pictorial Supplement to the Bristol Phoenix* that when I walk around town I can see both what is there and what preceded it. One of Bristol's first houses, for instance, a clapboard whose walls were stuffed with eelgrass for warmth, stayed on its foundations long enough for a photographer to record it around the turn of the century. It's more vivid to me than its replacement, an asbestos-sided cottage with a wavy aluminum awning over the front door.

First stop, the auditorium. It's white-walled and high-windowed, with portraits of S. Pomeroy and Theodora on either side of its shallow stage, and the seats are green leather with the Colt crest stamped in gilt on the back. The principal walks onstage. We rise. (Years later, at my first college assembly, I am startled when nobody rises as the president enters.) He greets us on this, the opening day. A bell rings. We're off!

Bzzzz. The buzzer is sounding and Ruthie, Joanie, Jeanne, Anne, and I are in our English class, where we will drowse over *Gammer Gurton's Needle.* Our teacher, a third-grade classmate of my dead Aunt Margaret (in their class photograph they are side by side, my aunt thin and watchful and my teacher with thick hair and a mouth like a rosebud), is the quintessential Yankee, dry to the touch. She is rumored to hand out A's as reluctantly as a miser hands out money. Eventually, however, she will hand them out to me, and even laughs a rare laugh when I give her a story about a rabbit who puts her ears in rollers for Easter.

Bzzz, and we travel the olivewood-paneled corridors to history class, where we flinch from the room's stench. The teacher's legs are ulcerated, and she has spread newspapers around her desk to catch the drip. Soon, though, we will take the stench and the drip and the newspapers for granted, just as we will soon take for granted her slow, halting walk to school and back. We are thoughtless, but perhaps that is a kindness.

Bzzz, and I pause for water from a marble bubbler over which is a marble plaque that reads "To thine own self be true." The only one of us to stay with the language after Guiteras Junior High, I am going alone to Latin class, to sit next to a window from which I can see Hope Street's hustle and bustle. "Look," somebody whispers as a descendant of S. Pomeroy Colt's emerges from Linden Place next door. "He's carrying his money bags over to the Industrial Trust." We believe it. Our notion of money has nothing to do with checks or stock certificates. As far as we're concerned those are dollar bills that S. Pomeroy's descendant is lugging across Hope Street in those two canvas bags, and maybe we're right. Ganny says the old Yanks still have the first dime they ever made.

The teacher usually stands by that window, her round face pinked by the morning sun and splitting into a gap-toothed grin. "Can you hear him?" she asks after reading us the Cicero that follows our ninth-grade Caesar. "Can you *hear* him?" We can. After we're settled into our seats there are no games or giggles in this room, no notes slipped from hand to hand. There is nothing here but Cicero speaking, and the sun ribboning our desks.

Bzzz, and I rejoin Ruthie, Joanie, Jeanne, and Anne for French class. The French teacher is lame, and lists when she walks. Miss C. is cherished, having taught so long that she is as much an institution as the Bristol/Barrington Thanksgiving Day football game and the Senior Reception. In fact, she was my mother's teacher too, and often the two of us meld in her mind's eye and she calls me by my mother's maiden name.

What little French she teaches is peculiar, but her conversation—and this is what our class is, one long conversation—is enthralling. When she isn't describing the Catholic ladies' college she attended a million years ago, she is talking about her great passion for France, a country which, *malheureusement!*, she will never see unless they build a bridge across the Atlantic Ocean because she is, *hélas!*, terrified of boats. Then she talks about us.

Thomas, the smartest boy in the whole school, is going to do remarkable things in science; and Anne has a genius for pronouncing French correctly; Ruthie is a born leader, and I? Miss C. puts a serious look on her small, pug-Irish face. "God has given Mary Lee," she says, "the gift of writing." When we leave her class we are twice as big as when we entered. But we have no French.

Forty minutes for lunch in the basement cafeteria! We buy the hot dish—our parents can afford the twenty-five cents it costs—but many of the Portuguese girls cannot. They are huddled uncertain in the girls' toilet, taking furtive bites of the sandwiches they have brought from home. How can they stand it, the constant flushing and the stink of disinfectant? My nose narrows. I reapply my Chen Yu lipstick; the peroxide streak I have put in my dark brown hair is canary yellow under the ceiling lights.

Bzzz. Time for chemistry lab and an hour in our rubber aprons, twiddling microscopes and duplicating aspirin and shuddering when the fumes from acid hitting acid spiral from our test tubes. We love chemistry class, the slumping on our stools and the casual walking around and no proscriptions on whoops and conversations. Above all we love the teacher, big and blond and forever frazzled. He is said to be witty, and God knows we will think him so. But how can one help but find hilarious a man who has been put on earth to keep a roomful of kids from setting themselves on fire with Bunsen burners?

Bzzz. Last class, up on the third floor in a room with a sloping roof, most of it a frosted-glass, chicken-wired skylight. We are in another of Miss Nerone's garrets, and she is whipping from easel to easel, cocking her head, squinting her eyes, framing the student's view of the bowl of fruit or the pitcher with the spray of bittersweet with a freckled hand. All the Italian boys draw very well—it's in their genes, she tells me—but I, being mostly Irish, will not be skilled in the visual arts. Never mind, she says, half-Irish herself. Nobody can talk or write like the Irish can.

Bzzz. It is two thirty, and school is over for the day.

We leave in a body, Ruthie, Joanie, Jeanne, Anne, and I. Our plaid skirts are switching over our rumps, and our white socks reach halfway to our knees. Textbooks have been added to the notebooks cradled in our left arms, and our ever-present purses are laid carefully over them. We are heading south for lemon Cokes at the Hope Drug, which is where we will go in the afternoon instead of Buffington's because the owner's son, Bobby, is in our class, and we are loyal. But before we step off the marble walkway, I reach out and pat the bronze girl who wears my mother's face.

Two afternoons a week, however, I don't head south with the rest of the gang. Instead I turn north, to the Bristol District Nurses Association and Miss Emilie Connery, who has called my house to ask if I would like a job helping her address envelopes for the infantile paralysis appeal. I am thrilled, but no more so than Papa. After supper on the night she called he sat me down in the living room and said "I'm proud of you, Lulubelle, to be earning your own money. You're going to be a scrapper, like your old man."

We go through the phone book, I reading out the Bristol names and addresses and Miss Emilie writing them down.

Maybe there is an easier way to locate possible donors but we don't know one, and we are happy as the shoeboxes we keep on a table next to Miss Emilie fill up with the fruits of our labor. Some days Miss Emilie steps into the room across the way so the district nurse can give her a liver shot; and always, about half-past three, she sends me to Buffington's for a coffee cabinet, which is Rhode Island's name for a coffee milkshake. "See you get Mr. McCaw, and see you tell him it's for me. He knows how I like them."

At five o'clock we shut up shop. Miss Emilie puts on her fedora and I stack my books and together we stroll down Hope Street. We are pleased with our output, and Miss Emilie has been further fortified by her liver shot and her personalized coffee cabinet. But that isn't why we have a certain strut, a certain . . . amplitude perhaps, as we pass the darkened five-and-ten, and Eisenstadt's, where the awnings have been rolled up for the night, and the shuttered jewelry store and barber shop.

Miss Emilie's taste in cabinets is known to Mr. McCaw and her skinny flank is known to the district nurse, and I am known to Miss Emilie since the morning I was born. It is because of my sharp eyes and her Palmer Method script that hundreds of Bristolians are going to pony up money for the infantile paralysis appeal. Miss Emilie and I aren't just drifting alone on the stream of life. We've got a mooring here. We belong to this town, and it to us.

Chapter Seventeen

As boys, Ganny's brother George had been famous for his softball game and her son John for having won a race swimming from the foot of Byfield Street to Hog Island and back, while the order he was supposed to be delivering for Newman's Grocery was spoiling in the sun. Ganny herself was famous for her baked beans, as famous as her cousin Emma was for her angel food cakes, and a neighbor, old Mrs. Church, was for not letting people enter her house by the front door until they were eighteen years old. Ralph Kinder was famous for having driven the Merritt Parkway to New York faster than anyone else in town, and his brother Joe was famous for once having landed his plane on Hope Street, up near Silver Creek.

Usually, however, fame was acquired in high school. Even so, it lasted a lifetime, although often it had more to do with potential than with realization. The girls' gym teacher, for instance, was famous for the fact that she would have been a tennis champion had she only had a proper coach and a proper court to play on. A former student of Miss Nerone's was famous for the fact that he would have been a great artist had he not died in World War II. A boy in my class was famous both for being a natural athlete and for being too lazy to live up to his gifts.

That Ruthie was going to be famous was obvious from the beginning of her career in the public schools of Bristol, Rhode Island. Ruthie would be famous for being popular. Not only was she voted into every office for which she ran, but the schools' musical director, the barrel-body who had made fun of me when I couldn't read notes in third grade, had chosen her to lead the Colt Memorial High School Band.

She was a glorious sight marching down Guiteras Field at halftime and up Hope Street on the Fourth of July, a long green jacket belted over her white skirt and a tall shako riding the rim of her glasses. The marshal's baton was heavy, and raised a callus between the base of her thumb and the base of her index finger, and she employed it as one would a plunger. Straight up, straight down, and never a toss above the head or a pass through an upraised leg.

"*Breeep!*" her whistle signaled. Down went the baton and off she'd go, trailed by ten or so band members, among them Norman, his lips flattened against the mouthpiece of his trumpet; Jeanne, her eyes close to crossed over her clarinet; and whoever was the fattest boy in school strapped to the big bass drum. Joanie was Ruthie's alternate, tall and poker-stiff and bending a stern Swedish gaze on her charges.

Anne had achieved fame, too, as a cheerleader. "Green and White fight/Green and White fight/Green fight/White fight/Green and white fight," she'd urge, her bowling-pin legs bouncing her high into the air. The cheerleaders wore thick white sweaters and short green skirts, and when they flew up their skirts flew up with them and showed their neat little green cotton underpants.

The cheerleaders looked good all the time, but never better than on Friday nights in winter, basketball nights, when parents, students, and boosters crowded the Andrews Gym, big and bright and smelling, irremediably, of sweat. The Industrial Arts teacher was there, famous for his four-syllable name. "Mr. Agatiello, whatcha doin' tonight?" we'd sing to the tune of "In the Mood." "Mr. Agatiello, whatcha doin' tonight?"

The coach was there, famous for having guided the team to the Class C championship. A pin-headed man whose legs turned out curiously from his hipbones, he was married to a woman who painted her lips well outside their margin. What with his invitational legs and her knowing mouth we thought them sexy. We thought they knew a thing or two. The high school principal was there, famous automatically. And I was there, famous only for turning in a lot of book reports.

During the half, Anne and the rest of the girls would swoop across the court, little skirts flashing little pants, to greet the cheerleaders for the opposing team. Standing in a circle, they bent their heads and exchanged what appeared to be deep, intensely female secrets. Then, suddenly, like flowers unfolding, they'd break loose from one another and run back, flushed and pretty, to their own sides.

Once a year, one night in midwinter, I too was out on that floor, standing before hundreds of Bristolians in a blue bloomer suit and waving Indian clubs in unison with Ruthie, Joanie, Jeanne, and Anne. I wasn't agile enough for rope-climbing, the trapeze, or the horse, but at least I was on the team.

In autumn I played field hockey, left half, on the big field in back of Colt, shin protectors buckled to my legs, hockey stick blistering my hands, eyes fixed on the small white ball as it appeared and disappeared in the stubby grass, in a light that was as bronze as the trees. We played till our lips and hands and knees were blue, and by the time we walked home the light, too, was blue, and dense and chill as the harbor.

On Saturday afternoons in fall a crowd moved slowly down High Street after the football game at Guiteras Field, and I moved with it, feeling as if our legs were powered by the same piston. On Thanksgiving morning Esther walked toward the Ferry alone because Diana and I were standing, our feet nearly frozen to the rimed grass, at Victory Field in Barrington, cheering on the team. The Barrington kids were stuck-up, we said, and their songs, we knew, put ours in the shade. "Viva la viva la viva l'amour. Viva la viva la viva l'amour. Viva la Barrington," they chorused, their blond heads glinting in the pale November sun. Once I had wanted classmates who looked like them—blue-eyed and bound for Princeton, Wellesley, Smith. Not now. Now I looked at the motley crowd that was the student body of Colt Memorial High School and found myself thick with love.

I would like to have had them all well behind me, the catechism lessons and the rustle of nuns' robes and priests' cassocks and the hiss of "myss-sstery" and "sssym-bol." But there was one more sacrament to be achieved. I had never been confirmed.

When the bishop of Rhode Island made his previous quadrennial visit to Bristol, Ruthie and I had been a few months shy of twelve, and thus too young for confirmation. Now we were the oldest students in the class that met every Friday afternoon in the dark basement chapel of St. Mary's.

My parents had been married in that chapel and now, over twenty years later, I sat there shivering in the damp while a priest warned us of the hardships awaiting Catholics in a hostile world. "When the bishop slaps your cheek," he said, "that slap will symbolize the blows you will experience in the defense of your faith." "Snubs" he should have said, I thought. It would have made the message more contemporary.

Just as we had run across the Common after leaving our First Communion class nine years before, so Ruthie and I ran across the Common after our confirmation lessons. It was darkening now as it was then, and the empty bandstand looked lonely as ever. Only this time we were running back to school, and the Friday afternoon dance.

The green leather chairs were stacked in the corridor outside the auditorium, and Perry Como sang "Kiss me once and kiss me twice and kiss me once again," while the girls with no boyfriends watched at the sidelines, and the boys with no girlfriends nudged one another or, if they were shy, studied the floor. My having a boyfriend made me seem popular, so I got to dance, raised slightly on my toes as Papa had taught me and stiff-arming my partner. I tried to hold myself back a bit when I danced with boys, to leave a little space between my stomach and theirs, but sometimes I couldn't and felt against my thighs a worm stirring, then struggling to escape. That was torture, and never more so than when it was Norman with whom I was dancing, Norman who put out a shy hand to mine when we were at the Pastime and who put a hesitant arm over the back of the glider when we sat on the porch. Norman of the clean, clean shirts and his older brother's after-shave. My small breasts had done this to him, my breasts and the backside that started rounding only a few inches from where he placed his scrubbed, short-nailed hand.

On a Sunday evening at the end of November I was finally confirmed, in a white dress borrowed from Miss Nerone's niece, who went to a Catholic school in Providence and needed white dresses for processionals and Maytime crownings of the Virgin Mary. My old First Communion veil, white tulle pendant from a kind of bicycle clip, sat oddly on my head, and the dress, because the niece was shorter than I, barely covered my knees. Some of the girls, though, the ones who went to St. Mary's Parochial School, were as dressy and radiant as brides.

We were supposed to take for a middle name the name of a saint we admired. My mother mourned the day she'd chosen Gertrude and Esther said she didn't know what was on her mind when she'd picked Genevieve, so I stuck with my baptismal name and was confirmed "Mary Mary."

Then, while the organ thundered and the incense eddied, we children of the church walked up the aisle of St. Mary's Church and out the door into the lobby.

The outer door was open, too, and the Common stretched before us, desolate and curiously romantic in the darkness. I was pure, pure as the sacraments could make me, and white from my underwear out. And never again would I have to sit in a classroom or a chapel while somebody tried to stuff my head with something that couldn't be taught. The last building block was in place.

Chapter Eighteen

I kept diaries. I cannot say I kept "a diary" because the term implies continuity. Instead I would write for a few weeks in a little spiral-bound notebook, misplace it, and start again a few months later with another spiral-bound notebook. Sooner or later I would misplace that one, too, and start all over again. Once I read an essay about socks, and how they seem as to give birth to one another. That's the way it is with my diaries. Whenever I am visiting 232 Hope Street, a corner of the attic or a drawer that hasn't been opened in years gives up another little spiral-bound notebook.

The girl who filled those notebooks with a curious hybrid of Palmer Method script and private school printing, was very fond of French words. "Who should meet me ce matin mais mon coeur?" she wrote about a boyfriend. She was worried about sex and concerned that she not receive a "rep," but safeguarded by her coldness. "Kissing doesn't bore me. It just doesn't affect me. Some parts of my emotions have yet to be uncovered, I can see." On the other hand, she wasn't really safe because she was determined to feel something. "I'm afraid I'm too curious. I want to see if anything will affect me, and it doesn't." Her determination, however, was somewhat sapped by her Puritanism. "I hope I never lose my head to the baser pleasures. Not that I'm not a base person—I am in many ways—but I hope I remain forever dead to these emotions. I may miss a lot. I don't know. I'm so confused."

Her relationship with Ruthie, Joanie, Jeanne, and Anne appear to be harmonious, although once she refers to "those harpies who call themselves my friends," and that with boys, tortured. "You know, Cantwell, you give me a big yack. In four weeks you have fallen for and away from three boys, and you all but threatened to commit suicide over one of them. Cantwell, don't be a boob. Don't believe a word they say. I mean it!"

Her most tortured relationship was with Norman. "I love him so, in spite of it all. It is no quick love of passion and glad moments. Instead my love brings misery and pain. It lies within not as warm and comfortable but as a stone upon my heart."

She went to the movies every Friday night, sometimes with Norman, but usually with Ruthie, Joanie, Jeanne, and Anne; and to dances at the Y.M.C.A., again with them. Having a boyfriend was not the same as having dates. The boyfriend part of it had to do with being walked home afterward. Dates, real dates, were only for the Junior Prom.

The linden trees in front of Colt High were in full,

AMERICAN GIRL

heartbreaking scent in May, in time for the Junior Prom, and on the great night the enormous lanterns outside the entrance were lighted. Friends and families of the Franks and Tonys and Sals ("Nobody can wear white jackets like the Italians can," Miss Nerone said) and Lucys and Theresas and Doloreses lined the marble entranceway to watch them promenading toward the massive mahogany door. It never rained, not once, and the air was like feathers.

My entrance—I always thought of it as an entrance, during which I would astonish with my glamor or, in the year I wore a pleated periwinkle blue crepe I thought Grecian, with my glorious austerity—was preceded by an afternoon at Mother's hairdresser, Mary Cappucilli. Blissful I was among the hiss of the shower sprays, the whine of the hairdryers, and the piles of *Photoplay* and *Modern Screen* while Mary rollered my straight hair and her helper, Angie, crimsoned my fingernails. Ganny and Gampa saw the hairdo first, then, head held stiffly so I wouldn't crack the glaze, I mounted the stairs to show Mother.

Supper was early and the bedroom still pink with sun when I put on my gown and Mother rummaged in her closet for her broacade evening wrap and in her top drawer for her beaded purse. At last I'd drift into the living-room and, spreading my skirts so they wouldn't wrinkle, sit. And sit and sit. No matter how well I knew my escort, usually someone with whom I'd had a Coke at the Hope Drug before my appointment with Mary Cappucilli, my knees were rubber and my palms wet.

The doorbell rang. We smiled—Papa, Mother, Di, and Esther shared the vigil—and the living room came back to life. The boy entered, a white box from Kinder's in his hand, and I would slide the corsage—gardenias, or, once, a raft of red roses that extended splintlike to my elbow—onto my wrist. Then down the stairs and out to somebody's father's car, and Ganny and Gampa peeking out the window.

A five-piece band blared from the auditorium stage; the girls smiled at one another over their partners' shoulders; the crepe paper hung in swags and balloons bobbed from the chandelier. This was the only time when it was okay to have a boy's arm around your waist, and to feel the length of him against the length of you. Sometimes the worm stirred, and then I'd extend my right arm slightly and try to back discreetly away.

By "Stardust" our skirts were crumpled, our feet were hurting in their unfamiliar heels and our cheeks were damp and reddened by hours of adhesion to our partners' cheeks. If our partner had a heavy beard, they were also somewhat chafed. My escort would help me into Mother's wrap, lifting my hair so it would clear the collar and sending, more surely than a kiss ever did, a tingle of sexuality along my spine. Shaken, I'd rustle into somebody's father's car and keep my eyes on the road and my hands in my lap as we headed for the Newport Creamery.

At the Creamery, Ruthie and Joanie and Jeanne and Anne and I spread our skirts along the booths and tossed our heads to display our mothers' earrings and anticipated the kiss, or kisses, that would end the evening. Norman kissed with flat, dry lips; Bobby, the boy whose father owned the Hope Drug, kissed wetter. J.B., who was older than the rest of us, had a mouth that smelled of tobacco. In three years at Colt High I was kissed by three boys.

One Junior Prom, however, ended differently from the others. The mother of one of the nicer boys (nicer meant somebody who lived on Hope or High Street and would go to college) gave a small party after the dance. She had been in my mother's class at Colt Memorial, just as her son was in mine, and was famous for her bridge luncheons and cocktail parties.

We wandered through her living room, suddenly strangers to one another, Ruthie in plaid taffeta and I in white tulle, and the boys in their white jackets. We sipped from little glass punch cups and plucked Vienna sausages from the "porcupine" Billy's mother had made by sticking them, on toothpicks, into an upended grapefruit half. If we sat it was only on the edge of the chair, and when we walked it was as gingerly as if we were treading ice. Our voices were soft and our laughter low, and I longed for a cigarette to punctuate my sentences. But of course I didn't smoke, none of the nicer kids smoked. This was going to be our world someday, this world of drinks and Vienna sausages and murmured conversations, and we swaggered a little bit, getting used to it.

That was the best evening, that and the night that again Ruthie wore her plaid taffeta and I wore the halter-necked white tulle that was my favorite evening gown to usher at the high school graduation. This night there were no worries about a doorbell not ringing or a boy dancing too close or of slipped shoulder straps and crushed skirts and smeared lipstick. Nor would I be crammed into a car, sitting on a boy's lap and miserable and guilty because I'd felt his penis swell beneath my thighs. Tonight Ruthie and I would come home as immaculate as we went forth.

After the gradution ceremony, when the last parent had left the auditorium, Ruthie and I hung around for a little while, watching the janitor pack up the folding chairs. By the time we started down Hope Street it was empty and a faint mist had come in off the harbor. When we got to St. Michael's Church Ruthie said "Shall we dance?" "*Mais oui!*," I replied and dropped a curtsey. Nobody saw us as we dipped and swirled and flung our arms to the sky because all Bristol was in bed.

When we got to 232 Hope Street we kept on dancing, she with Rhett Butler and I with Heathcliff, and both of us as giddy as if we'd been drinking spiked punch. One or two cars drove past the house, the light was on over the front door, and the fallen petals from the white rose bush that climbed Ganny's porch were like candles in the grass.

Chapter Nineteen

Gampa's bachelor brothers, Uncle Johnny and Uncle Jimmy, have given me luggage. Blue. Aunt Mame, Gampa's rich sister, a watch she bought in Switzerland when she made the Grand Tour in 1929 and a ring set with three small diamonds—one from Uncle Johnny, one from Uncle Jimmy, and the third from the engagement ring left me by Aunt Annie. Papa and Mother have given me a Smith-Corona portable in a maroon leather case. Ganny and Gampa, a card with a handkerchief and a ten-dollar bill tucked inside. I also have cards from Miss Nerone, Miss Munro, Miss Bosworth, Miss Emilie, and Miss Aida Connery and several of the Barrington crowd. I am about to graduate from Colt Memorial High School.

Any longer at 232 Hope Street and my case of the Bristol Complaint will be fatal. The harbor and the air and the trees will have snared me so firmly that I will never be able to leave town. I will never be able to see the world. "When you get out of Bristol . . ." Papa says. "When you get out of Bristol . . ." Miss Nerone says. I will never get out of Bristol if I don't do it while I'm young.

I have always hated three o'clock in the afternoon. At three o'clock *Our Gal Sunday* and *The Romance of Helen Trent* are over and my mother comes into the bedroom with an eggnog and says "You have to nap now or you'll never get over that cold." At three o'clock the light turns a funny yellow and Ganny plumps herself into her rocker to doze a little, and the faucet is dripping in the kitchen, and the clock on the mantelpiece is ticking and the dishes are draining by the side of the sink. At three o'clock Alger's Newsstand is empty because the oldsters are napping and it's too early for the schoolkids, and the Misses Osterberg are enjoying the pause at the Rogers Free Library. The ticket booth at the Pastime is closed and there's not a soul on the Common. If I don't get out of Bristol it will always be three o'clock in the afternoon.

When Mother sends me down to the front hall to snap the lock for the night, I feel the dark and indeed all Bristol pressing against the door. Let me thumb down the button on the lock, though, and they can't get in. Nothing can get in. Years later, when so many of its rooms are empty and the warriors who thronged them are present only in the dent in a mattress or a chip in a plate, I will still think of this house as a fortress.

But Papa wants me out of the house and out of Bristol. We have such plans! First, he wants me to do well in college because, he says, "I've always wanted to wear a Phi Bete key." We chuckle at the picture he'll make: Papa with a Phi Bete key dangling from the gold chain that always swags his stomach.

My junior year I will spend abroad, preferably at Trinity in Dublin, where I will see *The Book of Kells* and the bullet holes in the Post Office walls and walk on St. Stephen's Green. "You should know your heritage, Mary Lee, it's something to be proud of."

After college we're not sure what path I should take, but we think probably graduate school. I will study some branch of English literature and get my Ph.D.—"Always wanted one of those in the family"—and along the way I should marry some nice guy. My first son I will name Donovan, which was Papa's mother's maiden name.

Details, details. In the end the details don't matter. What matters is that I am going to see the world. I cannot wait to see the back of this town!

Papa knows as well as I do what will happen if I stay in Bristol and sleep in my own little bed forever. I will be like the S. sisters, wasting my sweetness on the desert air. Then I will dry up and drift down Hope Street like a leaf on the wind. Eventually I will end up sitting among the rocks at Union Street and teaching myself French and Italian. Sooner or later I will be what Bristol calls a character. "Get out," Papa says, "get out."

I want to go to a women's college, the kind where the students roll hoops on May Day and wear gray flannel shorts with boys' letter sweaters turned inside out, and visit Yale and Princeton on the weekends. And both of us want me to be some place where nobody's ever heard of my Uncle John. I have yet to meet him, but once I eavesdropped on Gampa and Ralph Kinder when they were talking about "Red," and I think I heard the words "cell block seven." Papa is the only one in the house who ever talks about him out loud. "One day God picked up a rock," he told me, "and your Uncle John crawled out."

I want to go to the place my father promised, the place where there'd be lots of people like me. Above all I want to be queen of England.

I have never aspired to be part of the Ferry crowd, and I never will. But by now I am a monument to antennae, all of them waving fiercely when they discern a snub. The day a boy from down the Ferry, one of the summer people, was riding me home from the yacht club on the bar of his Raleigh, for instance.

We were nearing 232 Hope Street when Gampa came along, an old shirt tucked into his khaki trousers and his loafers—my father's cast offs—floppy on his skinny feet. Judy, her rump wiggling, was pulling on her clothesline leash.

"You be careful on that bicycle, Mary Lee," Gampa called out.

"My grandfather," I said to the boy, and waved.

"Is that *really* your grandfather?" he asked, and his eyes chilled to blue marbles.

He had long rabbit teeth, and I longed to push them down his throat. I would have, too, if Papa hadn't told me never to let people realize that they had gotten to me. My anger was our secret.

Today, on this Thursday morning in mid-June, Ruthie and I are heading toward Andrews Memorial for the graduation rehearsal. Andrews Memorial is a big red-brick building across the street from Colt, and it houses the gym, and the model home for the girls whose career will be housewifery and the machine shop for the boys who will work with their hands. Papa was on the building committee for Andrews, and I thrill when I see his name on the plaque in the entryway—no S. Pomeroy Colt perhaps, but enrolled in Bristol's history anyway.

Ruthie and I are wearing old sweaters, old skirts, and scarves over our hair, which is in curlers. The idea is to look as rotten as possible so as to make tonight's transformation from grub to butterfly the more amazing. As we go by Kinder Florists, Ralph Kinder sticks his head out the door. "Congratulation, Mary Lee," he shouts across the street. Mr. McCaw, the druggist, says it, too, when we stop at Buffington's. Everybody's been saying it all week, and the yearbook picture of each and every member of the graduating class of Colt Memorial High School was in Tuesday's *Phoenix*.

The yearbook is lying on a table in the living room, autographed by most of my classmates and all of my teachers. Ruthie was *The Green and White*'s editor in chief;

Jeanne would have been its business manager if she weren't out of town for a year with her parents; and Anne and I were the literary editors. Together we have chosen quotations from Papa's copy of *An Anthology of World Poetry* to introduce each section and to run under each student's photograph. "These are the days of our youth, the days of our dominion . . . all the rest is a dream of death, a doubtful thing. Joy of joys for an hour today, then away, farewell," it says at the beginning of the senior class section. My throat swells when I read it aloud, and I feel powerful, as if there were a scepter in my hand.

Ruthie and I have chosen "No coward soul is mine,/ No trembler in the world's storm-troubled sphere" for Anne. Anne and I have chosen "A heart with which to reason and a head with which to contrive and a hand with which to execute" for Ruthie. (Ruthie doesn't look quite herself in the yearbook because the photographer made her take off her glasses.) My quotation, chosen by Ruthie and Anne, is from Louis Untermeyer: "A glow, a heartbeat, and a bright acceptance of all the rich exuberance of life." In the class will Ruthie has left a case of aspirin to her successor and I have bequeathed a girl in the junior class my leftover book reports. My passion for Norman is recorded for all time in the class prophecy: Anne, who wrote it, has me living in an old age home and knitting instrument covers for retired musicians.

It's been a busy year. Ruthie played the lead in the

senior class play, *Don't Take My Penny*, about a stagestruck girl, Penny Pringle, who wants to play the role of Dimity West in a movie to be made of a best-seller called *Stars in Her Hair*. I was cast according to type, I guess: My character, Penny's stuffy older sister Mavis, was in the tradition of Veronica Gladwyn. The cast picture—we are assembled on the stage of Guiteras Junior High, site of my performance in *Kitty Foyle*—is in *The Green and White*.

So are two pictures, one of the principals and the other of the chorus, of the cast of *Marianne*, the senior class operetta, which was set in Alguarra, a fictitious country in South America. Ruthie, Anne, and I are standing together in the chorus, wearing the Alguarran national dress: off-the-shoulder blouses, dirndl skirts, white socks, and loafers. The martinet who was musical director for the public schools, the woman who made fun of me in the third grade and whom I will never, ever forgive, directed both the play and the operetta, and choreographed the latter as well. "Now girls," she barked, "link your arms. Now take two steps to the left and give a little low kick with your right foot. All right? Now, two steps to the right and a little low kick with the left. Now, move again to the left, kick, two steps back to the right, kick. Now, *two* to the right and kick and back and two to the left and kick and back. Got it? Okay!" At intermission one of the Alguarran caballeros played "Over the Waves" on his accordion, and at midnight the streets of Bristol rang with the Alguarran national anthem.

It's warm in Andrews this morning, and strange to be walking on the gym floor in regular shoes. This floor is precious as rubies, and unsneakered feet are allowed on it only on Graduation Day. It's noisy, too, because the custodians are setting up the folding wooden chairs and the martinet is nipping at our heels, trying to get her sheep in line for the processional. We will march in two by two in alphabetical order. Then those on the left will turn and mount the left-hand stairs to the stage, and those on the right will go up on the right-hand side. Seeing that my name begins with C, my seat is in the first row.

Up and back, up and back we march until our halting, flat-footed steps are absolutely on the beat of "Pomp and Circumstance." Then we practice, over and over again, our three musical offerings—"Vienna, City of My Dreams," "Panis Angelicus," and our finale, "The Battle Hymn of the Republic." We are singing "Panis Angelicus" because this year is the year for a Catholic hymn. Next year is the Protestants' turn, so the hymn will probably be "A Mighty Fortress Is Our God." At high school graduation the religious niceties are as rigorously observed as they were in grade school, when we proferred our alternate endings to the Lord's Prayer.

The light is the color of golden syrup, and the air is getting thick. It's time to amble home, time for an afternoon nap and a long soak in the tub and, finally, the putting on of the white organza dress that Papa bought me at Saks Fifth Avenue in New York. It is hanging on the closet door now, and is the last thing I'll see as I sink into sleep.

The dress has a double Peter Pan collar, tiny covered buttons, long puffy sleeves, a white sash and a big full skirt, and it falls over me like a cloud. Under it I am wearing—drawn on as slowly and as punctiliously as a bullfighter draws on his suit of lights—a white cotton bra, white cotton underpants, a white cotton garter belt, a pair of my mother's nylons, a white cotton petticoat and gold sandals that we have bought at A.S. Beck, a rather low-class shoe store in Providence, because it doesn't do to spend good money on shoes you're only going to wear once or twice.

Mother gave me a bottle of Prince Matchiabelli's Wind Song cologne for Christmas, and I have worn it only to dances. Now I dab some behind my ears and on my wrists, and Papa, having read of this trick somewhere, suddenly asks Mother where she keeps the Vaseline. "It's supposed to make the eyes lustrous," he says, and slicks some on my lids.

The doorbell rings. It's Ruthie, come to get me for the ceremonial walk uptown. We look like brides, and along about State Street we join a host of other brides—and grooms—all of us converging on Andrews. As we walk through the entranceway we are handed our flowers—Colonial bouquets: tea roses and baby's breath furled into lacy paper doilies and twin to those young Bobby Kinder used to present to the birthday girls.

Just before the ceremony starts, as we are standing near the plaque that bears my father's name, my Uncle Johnny arrives with his handyman, Happy. They have driven down from Warren in Uncle Johnny's auto—a 1929 Chrysler Imperial because my relatives are no more inclined to throw out cars than they are to get rid of furniture—just so Johnny can rush in, red-faced and stocky, to shake his grandniece's hand. I am proud to have an uncle who thinks nothing of traveling four miles for a moment's meeting, and even prouder that mine is a family that exchanges gracious handshakes and not sloppy hugs.

The martinet nods from the doorway, and—at last!—I stare at her coldly. "Dah dah *dah dah dah* dah" sounds from the gymnasium and in we march, as slowly as if we are following a hearse, the boys in white jackets, the girls in white dresses, and the Colonial bouquets trembling in damp hands.

We go up the stairs as lightly as shadows, take our seats as gracefully as kings and queens take their coronation chairs. The class president will greet the audience of family and friends "to whom we owe so much." I have already heard the valedictorian's and salutatorian's speeches, because they had to recite them at rehearsal. Both boys, both good at math, they are going to college. The principal will hand out the athletic trophies, and Ruthie, we all know, is getting the school's highest honor, the Walsh Memorial Medal, for being "a leader in the better ideals among students, of sterling integrity and character, truthful and commanding respect." The superintendent of schools, at whose wedding Papa was an usher, will give us our diplomas. Till then, except when we're singing, I can relax.

Tomorrow night is the Senior Reception, to which I am going with Norman, who has my number now. A few weeks earlier he took me to Providence on the bus, to buy records, and I was thrilled because wandering around the city with a boy struck me as illicit. But we quarreled, we are always quarreling, and he said, "The trouble with you, Mary Lee Cantwell, is that nobody will ever measure up to your father."

To the Senior Reception I will wear, as custom dictates, my beautiful white graduation dress. The dance is for seniors and their escorts, faculty and parents only, and I am looking forward to seeing Papa in black tie and Mother in one of the little bellboy jackets *à la* Schiaparelli and long black crepe skirts she wears to dances at the country club in Barrington. Norman has no rhythm so I plan to dance a lot with Papa, partly because he is, as all heavy men are said to be, light on his feet, but mostly because bliss for me is now and ever shall be being in my father's arms.

But that is not for another twenty-four hours, and now I am trying to see beyond the footlights to where Ganny and Gampa, Esther, Mother, Papa, and Diana are sitting. Miss Nerone is out there as well, Miss Nerone, who has determined where I am to go to college. On the day that I got my acceptances—one for the school for which Papa and I had always planned, the other from a school to which I applied because I'd seen an article on it in *Life* and liked the way the girls dressed—I ran into her in front of Kinder's. "I hope you're going to ———," she said, naming the second. "It'll give you a little sophistication. You're enough of a bluestocking as it is." Then and there I settled on the school with the girls who wore sailors' middies, and thus do we make the great decisions in life.

Behind me several girls are crying, one of them because her white dress hides a tiny bulge and she has to get married next week. Some of the boys are red-eyed too, and honking loudly. On Monday they've got to start looking for jobs. "I forgive you," I say to myself. "I forgive you for pulling up my dress to look at my underwear and calling me 'Teacher's pet' and throwing stones and never choosing me for the softball team. Were it not for you, I would not be the person I am today." I can afford forgiveness; I am leaving town. I am giving Bristol the back of my hand.

The martinet raises her hands slightly, palms up. We stand, careful not to let our chair legs scrape the stage. "City of love and sparkling wine," we sing. "You're such a part of this heart of mine." Unbeknownst to me my heart bounds over the edge of the stage and rolls up the aisle, out the door and south on Hope Street until, finally, it comes to rest on the pebbly beach at the foot of Union Street. Where it will stay, as it turns out, forever.

AMERICAN GIRL

A little later we follow it, Ganny and Gampa and Esther, Papa, Mother and Diana and I. We are walking slowly, in deference to Ganny's rheumatism, and Gampa looks very tall and thin beside her. He is wearing his best suit, brown with a thin stripe, and the tie Diana picked out for him. Ganny is wearing her best dress, purple crepe, with her jeweled-basket brooch pinned at its neck, and one of her bowed and fruited hats sits squarely on her head. Papa looks tall, too, and portly, in striped seersucker with a bachelor button bouttonière. Mother and Esther are on either side of him, exactly the same five-foot-two, eyes of blue in their pretty prints. Diana is wearing a cotton dress, and her long, heron's legs end in white socks and loafers.

In less than three years two of these people will have been folded into coffins, and Ralph Kinder will have woven a blanket made of red roses for each of them.

Tonight, though, we are all together, walking down Hope Street while a breeze sighs through the lindens, the maples, the elms, the oaks, and the horse chestnuts. Aunt Margaret is with us, too, and King Philip, and Ganny's cousin who stuck her hand into a box of sand and came out with a lump of dirt.

The houses are stiff and silent in the dark. My dress is softly brushing my stockinged legs, my garter belt is tugging at my hipbones. My ears are sharp as a fennec fox's and my eyes as large as a lemur's. I am launched!

Afterword

A few years ago we seven met again, on an equally formal
occasion. Gampa, wearing the brown suit he'd worn to my
high school graduation, was under the grass, next to Papa,
who was dressed in one of his Brooks Brothers pinstripes.
Ganny was about to join them, in mulberry-colored crepe
accessorized with a long-stemmed pink rose. A little boy,
Aunt Annie Clark's great-great-grandson, had put it in the
box just before the undertaker fastened the lid.

Mother, Esther, Diana, and I were above the grass,
standing by the brilliant emerald carpet—was it Astro-
turf?—that framed Ganny's grave, not far from a head-
stone that read MARGARET. It's the only marker in the entire
family plot. My mother's family doesn't set much store by
headstones, nor by ritual either. The puritanism of the old
Yanks among whom they were raised rubbed off, I guess,
and left them streaked with granite. Myself, I'm streaked
with Irish moss, which is why Mother and Esther were keeping an eye on me. I can't be trusted not to cry.

MARY CANTWELL

At breakfast, before we left for the funeral parlor and a few prayers by Ganny's bier, Esther told her husband that it didn't matter who said the funeral mass, that it was the service alone that was important. He is a Congregationalist, acquired when she was fifty-seven and he sixty-six, and although we have never known him to go to church he thinks all things Protestant superior. Especially Protestant funerals, which are, he claims, cozy and comforting. "You and your old Congregationalists," she barked. "Think you know everything."

But when a gigantic black man, a Nigerian who spoke in a singsong, strode out in front of the altar, Esther's jaw dropped. Who would have thought the rector of St. Mary's would have left the job of burying his oldest parishoner—Bristol's oldest resident, in fact—to a priest who was just passing through? Not only that, but Ganny's ancestors were St. Mary's first parishoners, part of the group that had to row across the harbor to hear mass before the church was built. Ganny never knew a black man in her life, except for the one who used to ride the Jewish ragman's truck, and now here she was in a stranger's hands. "The next time they pass the basket at St. Mary's," Esther whispered, "they can forget about getting anything from me."

"What can you expect?" she said later, forgiving the rector of St. Mary's and, indeed, the passage of time that was taking us all down into some soon-to-be-forgotten sump. "There's hardly a person in Bristol who can remember who anybody was now. And, besides, today it's the Portuguese that are running the town."

Our Portuguese grocery boy is buried in St. Mary's Cemetery, killed by trichinosis (he'd eaten homemade *chourice*) at fifteen. He had wild blue eyes that seemed to roll around the kitchen, and for weeks after he died I saw them skittering about the walls and ceiling. Diana's best friend is in St. Mary's, too, a little girl with banana curls and peach-colored skin who looked like wax fruit in her coffin. So is Miss Nerone, in green wool, with a rosary looped through her fingers.

I could walk up and down these rows pointing to a neighbor here, a teacher there. I could do it at North Burial Ground as well, where Miss Bosworth is lying with the watch that belonged to her father on a chain around her neck. And at Juniper Hill, where the older S. sister, who grew tired of waiting and lay down under her car next to the exhaust pipe, is now awaiting the Resurrection. All Bristol is an archaeological dig to me.

My stratum is not yet filled in. Once it is it will represent, I suppose, a kind of Mesozoic Era. The dinosaurs, the old Yanks, were dying out and the flowering plants, those sturdy Mediterranean and Lusitanian blooms, were starting to flourish. But my family's shards are puzzling. Neither old Yanks nor new émigrés, we're hard to classify.

When I am under this grass, toe to toe with Indian bones at last, I will finally have achieved my old goal, to be indissolubly a part of Bristol. But not the part of Bristol I'd prefer. Like my father, who disliked St. Mary's Cemetery, up near the Back Road and sweltering in the sun, I prefer North Burial Ground. Or if I had the money and connections, Juniper Hill, which is as beautiful a garden as there is in town. Oh well. Papa used to say that Protestants always did get the best seats in the house.

After the Nigerian intoned his last singsong and the bearers had tossed their gray gloves onto the top of Ganny's coffin, Diana made a beeline for the back seat of the limousine as determinedly as she used to make a beeline for our tricycle. "Diana," I said firmly, "since I am the older and thus Miss Cantwell, and you are the younger and thus Miss Diana, it stands to reason that you, and not I, should ride on the jump seat." "Oh Mary Lee," she sighed. "You never change!" Then she giggled, and Mother turned on us a deep blue frown.

When Gampa and Papa had their wakes, the baskets and bouquets went all the way from the front hall into Ganny's two parlors; and Mame Lannon had her hands full accepting the cakes and macaroni salads and baked hams that came in by the back door. Hundreds of visitors filed in, in a cloud of 4711 Cologne and dusting powder, past the receiving line that was Mother and Esther, Diana and me. Then they peeled off to talk to Ganny who, too old to stand that long, sat in her rocker, moved for the occasion from the bay window to her bedroom.

First it was Gampa who lay in the bay window, his long

ivory-colored hands curled around his ivory-colored rosary. A night or two after he dropped dead—midway between his bed and the bathroom—I dreamed that he sat up in his coffin. "Gampa, I love you," I cried, but he lay down again before I could finish the sentence.

There was time to say it to Papa, though, or, rather, he said it for me. Six months later, when I was home from college between semesters, he took me out to Ganny's kitchen and made me watch while he sterilized a syringe and shot some morphine into his thigh. He wanted me to see that he was in charge, that he could manage the cancer that would have him dead in May.

"I've had some bad luck, Mary Lee," he said, "so I'm not going to be around much longer." The ceiling light was bright on the white enamel table, I remember, and the water in which he'd boiled the needle was still giving off steam. I looked at my father's thin white thigh—I had never seen his legs before and now his bathrobe was askew—and began to cry. My father winced.

"Please, please don't do that. It makes it worse. Don't say anything. You don't have to. I know how you feel about me." That was all that had to be said, really, by either of us.

So, streaked with Irish moss though I may be, I didn't cry; and when I stood beside the pretty trench, all fake green grass and heaps of flowers, into which his coffin was about to be lowered I was as granitic as my relatives. Serene, too, because I believed that now I was cloaked in him, that now he would never leave me. In truth, as I found out, I was cloaked only in the curious peace that attends the visitor to the graveyard.

Ganny's funeral was different from Gampa's and Papa's. At one hundred and five she had outlived all of her own generation and most of her daughters', and there were few left who knew her well enough to say good-bye. That's why we buried her from the funeral parlor and not from home, and why the only time I saw her in her coffin was on the morning of her burial.

But I had seen her a few months earlier, up at the nursing home. The cheerful young nurses called her Mag, which only Gampa had ever dared do, and kept her clean and polished. She was reminiscent of a bird by then, her nose a little beak and her wisps of hair tied back in a twist of scarlet yarn, and all that was left to show she'd been plump were her fat little feet in white anklets from the five-and-ten. Ganny's mind never wandered, but she kept long silences. "Waiting to die," she told me, "is very tiring."

Still, even Ganny dreamed. "I had a hummer last night," she told me. "I dreamt I was back on Pearse Avenue with my uncles and my aunts. Oh I tell you, Mary Lee, I was digging like a good un'." I, too, dig like a good un'. Too much, perhaps.

Several of the neighbors came in for cold cuts and sherry and to murmur "Mrs. Lonergan was a wonderful old lady" and "You'll miss her," but by the time Ruthie came to drive me up to Providence the house was as quiet as it was on the afternoons when Ganny and I sat in the bay window and watched the Hope Street parade. Downstairs hadn't changed at all. The late afternoon sun was striking the steel engravings, and dust motes were suspended in the beam. I was suspended, too, somewhere between mourning and memory. "If you don't get a hustle on, Mary Lee," my mother said, "you'll miss that train."

She didn't want me to leave. She never wants me to leave. But when I'm finally out the door, she's glad to see me go. It isn't very peaceful having me around. My husband used to say I had no serenity. She puts it more simply. She says I can't sit still. That I can't light anywhere, that I always have to be on the go. That's true. In my whole life I've never found a comfortable chair.

Ruthie took the route my parents took the night I was born: past Guiteras Junior High and Fort Hill and Collins Pond. Collins Pond is buried now, drained for a housing tract, and we hear the ranch houses and split-levels that replaced it have damp basements. Serves them right, we say. We miss Collins Pond and are sorry that nobody goes sledding on Fort Hill anymore, and would be sad to see the Pastime Theater, now the Bristol Cinema and desperate for customers, close its doors.

On the whole, however, Ruthie is not as nostalgic as I am. She doesn't have to be. She married one of the Catholic Connerys and never left town.

Did I? In my voice I can hear the voices of my family, my schoolteachers, the neighbors, all braided into one unmistakably Yankee tone. And once, when I was walking west with my then-young daughters, I sniffed that ummistakeable low-tide scent that comes off the Hudson and said, "Doesn't that smell like home!"

"Mother," my older daughter said, "this *is* home."

Ruthie and I talked while we waited for the train to pull in from Boston, but about what I don't know. Whenever we meet, even after months of separation, we just seem to pick up from wherever we left off. But we are both discreet, secretive even. Some people would say that's a loss, but I say it's a gain. We've been friends for so long that we have to use words only for the nonessentials. The rest we can say without ever having to open our mouths.

In a few hours I would be in the place my father promised, the place where there'd be lots of people like me. I have lived there a long time now, longer than I lived in Bristol, and for much of it I've been happy. But often when I'm out walking, when I find myself on, say, Fifth Avenue on a summer afternoon, I am puzzled. Then I ask that old friend with whom I am forever chatting, "What is Mary Lee Cantwell doing in this place?" The old friend doesn't answer.

I like this place. Sometimes I even love it, especially in early fall when the setting sun is poised midway between the old brick houses on either side of my street and that salty breeze has come up off the Hudson. I love it, too, when I take a cab through the Upper West Side late at night and those great old behemoths of buildings loom out of the dark like prehistoric monsters. Then New York is everything that Papa, for whom it was Ilium, said it would be.

Even so, it is not my country. My country is 200 miles away by Amtrak, and all it would take is the sale of an apartment and the packing up of some books and furniture for me to live there again. But if I did I suspect I'd be another Belle Bosworth butterflying my way around town.

I can see myself now, walking down Union Street toward 232 Hope after an evening at Ruthie's. The salt scent would be coming up off the harbor and the trees would be hanging heavy in the darkness. I'd move out toward the road as I passed the privet-hedged vacant lot next to the Tingleys' house because I've always feared that someone was lurking there. I'd reach out and touch Miss Munro's house as I always do because I know the brick came to Bristol as ballast and I like to imagine who touched it first. I'd hear the water lapping at the foot of Union Street and remember how I howled for Heathcliff. Then I'd look up toward the second floor of my house and see the lights still on: my mother up and worried because her child wasn't home.

There'd be no young man with hurt, trusting eyes. No daughters. No New York. No Mary, really, only Mary Lee. It would be as if nothing had ever happened, as if nothing had ever changed. Bristol, my Bristol, would blot out everything that came after it. No, the only way I can go forward—to where? I don't know—is to keep on running away from home.

About the Author

MARY CANTWELL is a member of *The New York Times* editorial
board, and won Scripps-Howard's Walker Stone Award for
editorial writing in 1986. She has also written frequently for
other departments of the *Times*, and was the author of the
"Close to Home" column.